2.0d

ANTIQUE JADE

Cassell Publishers Ltd
Artillery House, Artillery Row
London SW1P 1RT

Translated by Francis Koval from the Italian original
Antiche giade

British Library Cataloguing in Publication Data
Luzzatto-Bilitz, Oscar
Antique jade. — (Cassell's styles in art).
1. Jade art objects — History
I. Title II. Antiche giade. *English*
736'.24'09   NK5750

ISBN 0 304 32155 9
Printed in Italy by Gruppo Editoriale Fabbri, Milan

Oscar Luzzatto-Bilitz

ANTIQUE JADE

CASSELL
LONDON

INTRODUCTION

In the minds of Western peoples the very word 'jade' tends to evoke fascinating images of the fabulous Orient. Strangely enough, the word has in reality a somewhat pedestrian European origin.

As far back as the 14th century, Marco Polo, returning to Europe from his travels, told of the vast numbers of trinkets and ornamental objects which he had observed at the court of the 'Great Chan' in China. He described these objects as being most skilfully carved from some extremely hard stone which was pleasing to the eye because of the variety and delicate loveliness of its colourings. Here then was probably the first European knowledge of jade. Without doubt, however, the first to import jade to Europe were the enterprising Portuguese sailors and merchants who established regular commercial relations with China in the 16th century.

In fact, on their arrival in Canton in 1517 the Portuguese caravels under the command of Fernào Peres de Andrade were received by the local population with great cordiality, though some time later the brother of Fernào, in command of other vessels, provoked ill-feeling because of his overbearing conduct and the acts of piracy he committed against peaceful Chinese merchants. Even so, forty years later Portugal was given the right to purchase a tiny peninsula at the mouth of the Canton River. It was here that the Portuguese built Macao, the first bridgehead for commercial exchanges between China and Europe, which rapidly developed into a prosperous settlement. The export of jade objects was then conducted in secrecy and was not devoid of danger. Not only was jade considered by the Chinese an article of exceptional value (even more precious than gold); they also attributed to the mysterious stone some qualities of a magical and curative nature. Hence the strict prohibition of its export.

Since time immemorial jade had been one of the main articles offered annually as a tribute to the Emperor of China by 'barbarian' princes of the borderlands in an endeavour to ensure his protection in case of conflict with neighbouring tribes, or simply as an object of barter for which silk was obtainable.

The attraction that jade has exercised through the ages has obviously been due to its exceptional hardness, which makes it impervious to damage although very difficult to work. On the other hand, its fascination derives from its subdued smooth brilliance which—according to the prevailing colours—can be redolent of the deep waters of a mountain lake or of the mistiness of a distant summit.

The same Chinese character 'Yü' that stands for 'jade' has also the meaning of 'jewel' or 'treasure'. Moreover, the stone has always been credited with certain healing properties. In particular, by simple contact with the skin it was supposed to ward off kidney diseases and to ensure regular urinary functions. This curious legend followed the mineral to Portugal, where simple people readily accepted the belief and consequently used the name 'pedra de mijada' (urinary stone). Hence—through an understandable corruption of words—the stone from distant China emerged as 'jade'.

It is a curious fact that two centuries later—when the first classification (in Latin) of minerals was undertaken—the mineral in question was christened 'lapis nephriticus', which led to the present-day scientific name of 'nephrite' (from 'nephros', the Greek word for the kidneys).

In fact, the term 'jade' does not clearly define a strictly determined substance with constant characteristics. Genuine jade—known to the Chinese under the name of 'Chên Yü' for some forty-five centuries, since the Neolithic Age—is undoubtedly a calcium-magnesium silicate with the hardness degree of $6\frac{1}{2}$ according to the Mohs Scale (established in 1820); and this can be considered the classical nephrite. Various other minerals, usually softer but in some cases harder, have been and still are called 'Yü' or 'jade' by Europeans. The one among them most nearly resembling jade is a kind of stone known as 'serpentine'. In one variety found in China this mineral exceptionally reaches the hardness degree of 6, which is near to that of quartz, fixed at 7.

On the other hand, all the modern imitations exported via Hong Kong by wagon-loads and sold to credulous buyers all over the world as jade—usually in the shape of elegantly carved statuettes—are nothing but a sort of alabaster or translucent green fluorite, soft, easily carved with simple iron tools and therefore of insignificant value.

In the Neolithic Age, even before the discovery of metals, the carving of jade was current in China, as archaeologists have proved. The technique used by the Chinese craftsmen of the time was admittedly primitive, and yet revealed their innate intelligence and practical inventiveness. The cutting and shaping of jade was executed by hand with the help of a bone or bamboo stick, while the surface of the stone was covered with greasy ointment mixed with abrasive powder made from crushed garnets. Round holes were bored with a tubular tool made from an animal bone or a bamboo stick cut at a slant and sharpened with stones. This tube was made to rotate by means of a string wound round it and kept taut by a wooden bow. The to-and-fro movement of the little bow kept the hollow tube turning while pressure ensured close contact with the grease that contained the abrasive powder.

This primitive drill has probably some similarity to tools used in more recent times, and of which literary descriptions exist: a hollow cylinder made of bone or bamboo stem, turning on a smooth vertical pivot and kept rigid at the top by a wooden framework.

With the emergence of bronze implements in the 15th century BC and then of iron tools almost a thousand years later, the bamboo sticks were of course replaced by metal tubes. The general method of work, however, remained unaltered; and so it is easy to imagine how agonisingly slow the process was.

Still, in ancient records dating back to times in which such documents were usually adorned with fantastic legends, time and again reference is made to a wonder-knife called 'K'un Wu' which allegedly cut through jade as if it were chalk. The persistent repetition of such references leads us to believe—even allowing for the typically Chinese tendency to exaggerate—that there must be some truth in these statements and that in the distant past there indeed existed a more efficient tool than a pointed rod, even of metal. It would be logical to deduce that this might have been an iron tool with a diamond or corundum tip firmly embedded at one end.

According to legend, Yü the Great, the founder of the first Chinese Hsia Dynasty (towards the end of the 3rd millennium), was already in possession of one of these marvellous instruments. This seems absolutely impossible, since it is inconceivable that a diamond tip could be embedded in anything but a metal socket. But copper, the very first metal discovered by the Chinese (and by other peoples too) appeared in China only towards the middle of the 2nd millennium. An occasional import of that metal from the Near East, where it was in use before, is highly improbable since it is not borne out by archaeological findings or mentioned in traditional records.

A passage translated by Laufer from an ancient

text brings up the subject in connection with Mu Wang, the fifth king of the Chou Dynasty, a character surrounded in Chinese literature by a galaxy of strange legends. When this ruler conducted an expedition at the head of his army to establish contact with some alien tribes inhabiting the frontier regions of his kingdom, it is reported that he received in homage from the ruler of these tribes a knife 'K'un Wu'. This report seems all the more credible in that the tribes, known as Jun, had in their territory vast deposits of iron ore and might have started quarrying from the 10th century BC onwards—a period roughly corresponding to the reign of Mu Wang. At any rate, if this instrument did in fact exist in such a remote period (which is by no means proved by archaeological finds), it must have been an object of exceptional value and surely not in general use. As a matter of fact, all the legends or early records mentioning such a 'wonder knife', refer to it only as the property of a sovereign ruler.

Even admitting the knowledge and use in those times of metal tools with diamond or corundum tips, it must be understood that this was a purely Chinese invention. If the Jun tribes were involved at all, their participation must have been limited to the supply of the metal part—since they only exported jade pebbles in their rough form, and there is no indication that they attempted to carve them. Hence the theory that they might have invented a carving tool for the shaping of jade seems somewhat absurd.

Laufer, who fifty years ago wrote the first European

book on Chinese jades (and quite an exhaustive one at that), is of the opinion that the Chinese used diamond tips for jade-carving from the 1st millennium BC. Although his book is still considered authoritative today, his assertion in this respect is based on his own translation of the word 'chin-kang', which is frequently associated in legends with the knife 'K'un Wu', and associated in Europe with what we know as 'diamond'. He neglected to consider a variety of other meanings attached to the very same Chinese character, which is also used for the description of several particularly hard stones, among which is the corundum. And the fact is that corundum, unlike diamonds, is normally found in China.

This ambiguity has probably come into being through the endeavour to keep the secrets of jade-carving in a few tradition-bound families who passed them on from father to son. Also the oily substance used, until fifty years or so ago, for the blending of the abrasive mixture figured prominently in strange tales obviously designed to draw a veil of secrecy over the whole procedure. Over the centuries it was always stressed in Chinese texts that the raw material, 'toad grease', was produced from toads killed in a special manner and in strictly defined circumstances. However, the grease in question has always been tallow from mutton or pork, melted and worked into a consistency similar to our own lard.

According to another popular misconception the 'toad grease' was supposed to soften the jade so that it could be cut more easily. Clearly, however high the viscosity of the ointment used, facility in carving hard stones by grinding them with metal implements (not to speak of bone or bamboo tools) depends not on the type of grease employed but on the quality of the abrasive powder.

To people unacquainted with Taoism and its complex mythology, this association of jade and toads may appear startling, since it establishes a strange connection between a precious stone of particular beauty and an animal that generally arouses repulsion among Western peoples. It must be remembered though that the Chinese peasants of ancient times were in no way prejudiced against the toad but, on the contrary, appreciated the little creature's ability to predict weather changes. Thus, in a primarily agricultural society it played an important part. Moreover, the toad figures in many Chinese legends.

One tells the story of Ch'ang Ho, the young and beautiful wife of a famous bowman of the legendary Emperor K'u. She was also called Hêng, meaning 'Crescent Moon'. Once during a sleepless night while she was watching the moon, an eclipse set in. Whereupon she took from the bedside her husband's mighty bow and saved the moon by shooting an arrow into the dark shadow that threatened it. Then she stole from her husband the jar containing the Elixir of Eternal Life (which was the Emperor's present to him for services rendered) and fled to the moon, where she was instantly changed into a toad. In this shape she lived in a magnificent palace in the sole company of the Jade Hare (Yü-t'u), who crushed beautiful jade into powder to make the Elixir of Eternal Life.

It is fairly certain that in the period between the 5th and the 1st centuries BC corundum or diamond tips were already used in drills which were still rudimentary, but developed to the extent that their rotation was ensured by pedal work, leaving the hands free. With simple metal implements it would have been impossible to produce the refined engravings typical of the period and the bracelets made of elaborately interlaced links carved out of one and the same block of jade. Infinite patience and superb craftsmanship were needed in order to carve these marvellous works of art with only the help of the primitive tools available. That is why the completed works aroused admiration bordering on awe and reverence, and why they fully deserved the name bestowed upon them which in literal translation means 'Works of Spirits'.

This method of work was extremely costly too, and not only because of the high value of the rough diamonds used for the drilling tips. One of the difficulties was that in those times no drill with interchangeable heads existed. Once the precious stone was firmly embedded at the end of the iron rod (which was in itself a difficult enough task), it was subject to rapid wear or it splintered, rendering the whole implement useless.

This technique must have been abandoned at the beginning of the Christian Era. It was revived in 18th-century China, but only for the purpose of engraving dedicatory poems and inscriptions in wonderfully minute and perfect characters, a task that could not be accomplished by any other means. This explains the almost complete absence in the intervening period of graphic indications which might have facilitated the exact dating of antique jade.

THE ORIGIN OF THE
JADE USED IN CHINA

It is reasonable to assume that until the 10th or 11th century BC the only source of jade was in the alluvial deposits of Turkestan, which means that the pebbles or stones in question were never very big. True, ancient records mention a legendary Emperor who had a flight of steps built of white jade so that he could reach the abode of his favourite mistress with dignity. It must be remembered, however, that the Chinese word 'Yü', used for jade, easily led to confusion since it also denoted the kind of Parian marble quarried in China. This was a comparatively rare mineral, used as a rule for the temples or palaces of sovereign rulers. Even there it was not used for the construction of the whole building (as the Chinese always preferred timber to stone) but simply for outside stairs or for bridges which linked islands in artificial lakes, and so on.

One more proof of the confusion caused by the use of the ambiguous term 'Yü' is supplied by the Chinese pharmacopoeia, which prescribed the oral administration of pulverised jade for various ailments. Now there is no doubt whatsoever that genuine jade could not be assimilated by the human organism without causing serious illness or even death. Hence the deduction that the substance employed as medicine must have been powder of marble or magnesite, minerals which in their natural state have a consistency that is hard enough to be mistaken for jade but which are soluble in the gastric juices and capable of relieving excess acidity.

The first reliable reports of the extraction of jade from rock in Khotan date back to the 12th century. It is fairly certain, in fact, that very large blocks of jade were being carved then for the Emperors of the Yüan and Ming Dynasties, as well as for the Ch'ing, their successors. The most famous block, uniformly white, was shaped about the year 1410 into a pillar approximately six feet high; on it, for the benefit of posterity, the Emperor Yung Lo allegedly inscribed one of his long poems with his own hand. This exceptional piece of work is said to have been placed originally in the Imperial Palace in Peking, but it seems to have disappeared. As in the case of several big mountain-shaped jades kept in the same place, there is little likelihood that it was carried away by Chiang K'ai-shek and taken on his forced march to the south. The very size and weight of these unique works of art would have prevented him from doing so. Some rumours, vague and difficult to verify, circulating during the last war hinted at the presence of the precious pillar in Japan.

In Turkestan—a region which in the course of

history was in turn independent, a protectorate and a Chinese province—the quarrying of jade and its separation from the rock in which it was embedded has always been extremely difficult. Instead of using gunpowder, the quarry-men used to light big fires and keep them going in the immediate vicinity of a jade seam, so that the different rate of expansion caused by the heat in the actual seam and the surrounding ore produced cracks. Water was thrown on the strongly heated rock surface in order to enlarge these cracks, and then wedges of hardwood were driven into fissures with hammers. Such a procedure was not only very slow but also involved considerable wastage of the precious material.

The extraction of jade from the rockface did not, however, slow down the efforts to collect alluvial pebbles from riverbeds—a method still used today by riverside dwellers in some parts of Turkestan. Such tasks were generally assigned to women, who at the time of low water waded into the river, fished out the stones and threw them on to the banks, where men proceeded to segregate them. This custom of employing female labour for 'jade fishing' was dictated (like so many other peculiarities still prevailing in small localities in the interior) by a curious tradition of legendary origin. It was believed that the jade was intentionally hiding in the depths of the riverbed, emerging only in certain favourable circumstances, and that above all the precious mineral was susceptible to feminine attraction.

Despite recent rumours to the contrary, it seems

fairly certain that no jade is found in China proper. Since time immemorial it has always come from Turkestan, where the principal alluvial deposits exist in the rivers Yurungkash and Karakash, whose names in translation in fact signify 'River of Green Jade' and 'River of White Jade'. Both of them have their source in the mountain chain called K'un-lun.

A very ancient legend connected with Tao folklore seems to give poetic confirmation of the theory that jade was confined to the western regions. Once upon a time the 'Jade Queen' Hsi Wang Mu lived in her fabulous palace built on an inaccessible peak of the K'un-lun Mountains, attended by twelve princesses-in-waiting. Now, literally translated, Hsi Wang means 'Rulers of the West', and hence the whole name signifies the Queen (or Mother) of the Rulers of the West.

As a matter of fact, there exists, although historically not clearly defined, a vague mention of a race that inhabited the Turkestan regions now called Khotan and Yarkand and which was governed by a woman.

The story continues with the description of a journey made in the 10th century BC by the Emperor Mu Wang of the Chou Dynasty, who owned eight bewitched stallions—which enabled him to cover in one night the whole length of his immense empire. The aim of this journey was to establish a relationship with the above mentioned 'Jade Queen'.

Since all the legends that pass from one century to another possibly have a grain of truth in them, it is conceivable that this fable refers to an approach made by the Chinese sovereign to the western tribes with a view to obtaining a regular supply of jade. In those times Turkestan was, of course, independent and inhabited by a group known as the Jun.

The continuous interest in the jade country shown by the Chinese, and their wish to maintain friendly relations with its inhabitants, are somehow reflected in the continuation of the legend which deals with the love affairs of the mythical and immortal Queen Hsi Wang Mu.

About a thousand years after her affair with the Emperor Mu Wang of the Chou Dynasty, she fell in love with the Emperor Wu Ti of the Han Dynasty (156-87 BC). In order to meet him she descended from her palace, accompanied by five of her princesses— the latter being called 'Yü Nü', which in literal translation means 'Jade Girls'. In that period Turkestan, although semi-independent, belonged nominally to the great Han Empire; so this story may represent a poetic record of tribute-paying and submission by the Jun leaders to the Chinese Emperor. Wu Ti had become a fervent Tao supporter and believed in the Elixir of Eternal Life. It was from this period that the confusion regarding the qualities of jade existed. Jade was considered one of the Elixir's principal ingredients, and thus acquired an even higher value in the eyes of most Chinese people.

Towards the end of the 13th century Marco Polo, during his adventurous expedition to the mysterious Kingdom of Cathay (that is, the Chinese Empire at the time of the first Mongolian Emperor, Kublai Khan), certainly crossed Khotan. Having explored the markets where jade was exchanged for Chinese silk, he gives a vivid, if somewhat fantastic and imprecise, description of extremely valuable stones being loaded in abundance on the backs of camels setting eastwards. He does not, however, specifically mention jade (not known under this name then), speaking instead of chalcedony and 'diaspis' (probably jasper), two hard stones which were at the time well known to the Venetians. Thus he presumably bestowed on jade the names of these two.

Some years after the arrival in Portugal of the first jade objects from China, the Spanish conquerors of Mexico started sending back trinkets and statuettes made of a hard stone very similar to the Chinese jade collected by the Portuguese. It is not very likely that the Mexican Aztecs and Mayas held the same beliefs concerning the mineral's miraculous influence on urinary functions, and it is therefore more probable that the name 'pedra de mijada' or 'pedra de los riñones' ('kidney-stone') originated in Portugal. Because of the similarity of the two languages the term was soon accepted in Spain also, and spread all over the world in the corrupted form of 'jada'.

In actual fact, the majority of ancient jades of Central-American origin are not made of the genuine variety of this mineral ('lapsis nephriticus') as worked by the Chinese, but of a species which is still harder but of different chemical composition.

Central-American jadeite seen in thin slices under

the microscope presents a clearly crystalline structure, not a fibrous crypto-crystalline one like nephritic jade. Its greater transparency and shiny surface is in contrast to the muted brilliance of genuine jade.

Neither jade nor jadeite are subject to changes in their original state—that is to say when preserved from contact with air. Nevertheless, the slow process of oxygenation and carbonisation has caused obvious changes in the surface and in the structure of carved objects preserved in tombs or simply covered by earth. On the surface dull stains begin to appear and these tend to penetrate in depth. Of course, this process—which is improperly called 'calcification' and should rather be described as progressive deterioration—is so slow that it only becomes noticeable in objects aged at least a thousand years. The appearance of such symptoms depends largely on the conditions of the locality concerned, particularly on the humidity and other properties of the soil.

It is obvious that even if in this way the beauty of an object may be affected, the deterioration—signifying the great age of the object—may increase its value, turning it into a 'collector's item'. In recent times, the increasing demand for antiques has encouraged unscrupulous dealers to attempt to produce fraudulent imitations. Modern copies of very ancient jade objects are being made and then heated in high-temperature furnaces so as to produce an opaque surface layer which can easily deceive the layman's eye.

In all probability, in the pre-Columbian period the

ancient inhabitants of Central America used to quarry jade and jadeite from the rocks in the mountains of the Andes chains or in the Mexican Plateau. So far, no systematic research has been done to discover such mining localities.

More recently nephritic jade has been found sporadically in various parts of the world, and particularly in huge alluvial deposits in certain rivers of southern Siberia. This Siberian jade is generally dark-green, but with splashes of lighter green and blackish dots which are due to the presence of graphite in the composition of the mineral. In the language of the Chinese, its principal importers, this stone is called 'Spinach Jade'.

In a state of absolute purity both jade and jadeite should, in theory at least, be white. In reality, however, only jade, and not jadeite, is found in such a state, and not very often at that. White jade which is slightly translucent and opalescent is called by the Chinese 'Mutton-Fat Jade'. The wide range of colours found in nephritic jade is due to the presence in its composition of various metallic oxides or silicates. The most frequent colouring agent is iron. In the shape of ferrous oxide (magnetite) it endows the jade—according to the quantity present—with colouring that ranges from grey (most commonly encountered) to plain uniform black (very rare). Pale greyish-green shades ranging to near-black dark green at the other end of the scale, are due to the presence of ferrous silicate, which in very rare cases produces also a decisively blue shade. Ferric silicate, on the other hand, produces a colour that ranges from yellowish orange to dark brown. The highest value is attached to yellow jade when its colour is distinguished by clarity and uniformity.

The combined presence of different pigments leads to a great variety of colours and shades. Tiny traces of manganese produce the frequently found whitish jade with delicate pink or purple veins that are only just noticeable.

Among all these varieties the most common is that of light grey to green colour, called by the Chinese the 'Cabbage Jade'.

Very seldom, however, has the jade an even, uniform colour. As a rule, it displays clearly distinguishable veins or stains due to irregular distribution of metallic pigments in the body of the mineral.

Burma, the fabulous land of rubies, remains to this day the only country producing jadeite. In ancient times there was only one region that supplied jadeite: a valley where alluvial deposits of the stones had accumulated since time immemorial, forming a layer of considerable thickness. But about a century ago, quarrying of the precious material was started near the source of the Irrawaddy River. As for the date of the introduction of jadeite into China, there are different schools of thought. The majority view is that until the 18th century this stone was unknown in China, because the centuries-old conflict between the two countries had made regular commercial exchanges impossible until the peace treaty ratified by the Emperor Ch'ien Lung. On the other hand, reliable 12th-century texts mention a mineral called 'Yunnan Yü' that was being worked in the 'Jade Alley' of K'ai Feng, which was the capital of the Sung Dynasty from 1127. However, in the Yunnan (the extreme south-western province of China, bordering on Burma) jade is not found at all, so that the material in question must have been of Burmese origin.

A confirmation of this latter view may be found in a quotation from the famous philosopher Su Tung-p'o, a Chinese poet and politician who lived from AD 1036 to 1101. He thus describes renowned pieces of ceramics of his time: 'The red Ting cups have the brilliant colour of polished red jade.' Now it is a well-known fact that a brilliant red colour—due to the presence of chromium in the composition—is a characteristic of jadeite, but never found in genuine (nephritic) jade. Such colouring (and this also applies to the emerald green caused by smaller quantities of chromium and to the lilac colour due to traces of manganese) distinguishes jadeite at first sight from nephritic jade. There exists a vast literature on the life and personality of Su Tung-p'o, from which it is clear that he never visited Burma. And yet to give such a description he must have seen in China objects made of jadeite.

It seems indubitable, however, that until the beginning of the 18th century this mineral was used only on a small scale and considered rather as a sub-species of genuine jade. As such it was not highly esteemed until about 1750, since when its beauty and high value have gained general recognition.

There is a curious note in the memoirs of an 18th-century writer. He recalls that in his youth it was considered fraudulent to sell a piece of 'Yunnan Yü' (jadeite) pretending that it was genuine jade. Towards the end of his life he witnessed a startling increase in the value placed upon jadeite, so that in the end it attained higher prices than even genuine jade. Today's Chinese name for this variety is 'fei-ts'ui', which corresponds to the ancient word for the kingfisher found in South China. In Europe it is known as 'emerald-jade' and is used in jewellery, shaped in the same fashion, as a substitute for genuine emerald.

There still remains the unsolved problem of how the nephritic jade in its crude, uncarved state ever reached China (still in the Neolithic Age) between the 3rd and 2nd millennia; that it did so is proved by archaeological evidence found in tombs of the pre-Shang period. Many scholars assert that there has always been a source of jade in China proper since the era of the first Yang Shao culture of painted terracotta (c. 2200-1700 BC). Moreover, they affirm that the quality of jade dating back to the pre-Christian era and found in comparatively recent excavations is very different from that imported later from Khotan. It is highly probable, though, that this archaic jade has suffered changes in chemical structure through being buried for millennia in a humid atmosphere. Many objects have been analysed and proved beyond any doubt to be of nephritic jade.

True, several Chinese scholars refer to localities where in the past—according to them—jade was quarried. In this context it is only appropriate to reiterate that the Chinese term 'Yü' does not describe exactly a well defined mineral but usually embraces various species which are often similar in appearance and hardness, for example chalcedony, serpentine and bowenite. It seems therefore more plausible that well before the dawn of the Bronze Age, nephritic jade was being carried into China by semi-nomadic western tribes from the borderland of Kansu—where, after all, jade originating from before the 2nd millennium was found (in Pan Shan), and where the starting point of the whole Chinese culture of painted terracotta can be located.

MYTH AND SHAPE IN
ANCIENT CHINESE JADE

There is one classical object in the art of Chinese carving that has all through the ages—from the Neolithic era up to modern times—maintained a basic identity of form. This is the 'Pi'. It consists of a disc with a large central hole, and represents Heaven, in accordance with the sun cult derived from the age-old pseudo-religious beliefs of central Asian nomadic tribes, more ancient probably than the first nucleus of China's social order.

It seems obvious that for all primitive races the

heavens represented the highest deity, since they dispensed life-giving rain as well as the warmth that makes the crops ripen. As they are not always merciful, sometimes spoiling the harvest by prolonged droughts or ruinous downpours, and sometimes displaying their anger through thunder and lightning, it seems feasible that an instinctive cult of worship and supplication of 'Heaven' led to the first forms of religious ritual. Overpowering natural phenomena were obviously beyond the understanding of the simple minds of primitive races. As a result they proceeded to select from among themselves certain individuals who seemed endowed with the ability to function as intermediaries between Heaven, the mysterious deity, and common mortals. In an effort to bring the object of the religious cult nearer to the masses, these first Shaman priests created symbols— plastic representations of the object of worship.

One is bound to reach this inescapable conclusion by simply observing the primitive pictorial shape of the character denoting the sun, ⊙ , although some scholars of the subject offer other ingenious theories concerning the annular form of the Pi.

One of the oldest specimens of a Pi (at present in the collection of the King of Sweden) was found by Anderson in the Kansu and, according to his estimation, dates back roughly to the year 2000 BC. It is made of genuine grey nephrite, with pinkish specks due to ferrous impurities, and shows in parts opaque calcination. The contour is circular but with irregularities, while the central opening is absolutely perfect—which leads to the conclusion that it was produced with the help of a bone or bamboo drill driven by some kind of rotating device, however primitive it might have been. The majority of scholars deny that the Chinese had any knowledge of a rotating implement before the 1st millennium. This opinion, however, does not seem acceptable in view of the superb vases of painted pottery found with this Pi at Pan Shan in the Kansu. Since they are of globular shape and perfectly smooth, and the thickness of the shell does not exceed a few millimetres, they supply irrefutable proof that some kind of a potter's wheel or turning-lathe must have been used. For the last forty centuries the Chinese have obviously known how to effect a rotary movement by means of cords and pulleys, and therefore it is in my view impossible to deny *a priori* the existence of a primitive drilling device.

Another Pi, kept in the Academy of Arts at Honolulu, is almost identical with the above mentioned, but of a slightly later date, probably belonging to the First Shang or Pre-Anyang period (17th-15th centuries BC).

The Pi reproduced in Plate 5 of this book belonged to the famous Eumorfopoulos Collection and is today in the British Museum. It is of unusual shape and, as far as I can judge, is a unique specimen of its kind. It has the form of an axe-head or mattock (spade), with the usual central opening. It is my personal belief that it is a representation of Heaven-Earth dualism.

It must be remembered that for the ancient Chinese a separate and external earth cult did not exist. Earth was seen as the deity that regulated mankind's very existence. Next to the Sun god there was the Earth goddess, and their union was tantamount to the conception of Universe, the sole beginning of life.

In tombs discovered at Anyang, the last capital of the Shang Dynasty, various Pi's were found, embellished with engravings which range from simple semi-geometrical motifs to patterns repeating the complex symbol language of the ritual bronzes of the same era. This is an art which can hardly be called 'animalistic' because animals (or parts of animals) are represented in forms which are always unreal, fantastic and symmetrically formalised. The dominant figure, decorative and typically Chinese, is a monster associated in ancient mythology with the concept of rain or of water in general (its Chinese name is 'Kuei').

The myth of this Master of the Rains (or of the River) goes back to the dawn of history, although the name must have been coined in comparatively recent times (probably not before the 10th century AD). Parts of this dragon such as the tusks, claws and horns appear interlaced in a continuous zigzag pattern obviously shaped in accordance with a symbol language which has remained somewhat obscure to this day but which is not devoid of a peculiar fascination.

In the bronzes this art is, of course, much more refined and reaches its peak in the Shang period, .

approximately at the time when King P'an Keng transferred his capital to Anyang (in 1401 BC according to tradition, or in 1300 BC according to some modern historians). This move to the east was made in order to escape an attack launched by the Jun, the very race closely connected with the story of Chinese jade, since they were the chief suppliers. The name of the region in which the new capital was situated—the Yin Desert—was used by P'an Keng when he decided to change the name of his dynasty from Shang to Yin. This explains the seeming contradictions, likely to create a certain confusion among the less expert students of the subject, which occur in references made to this subject by modern historians.

The superiority of contemporary bronzes can be easily explained. These refined works of art were often produced with the cire perdu ('lost wax') technique. The use of this very soft material allowed for very subtle incisions with any kind of pointed tip, even a wooden one, whereas in the case of the extremely hard jade it was virtually impossible.

It is during this Shang period that a peculiar figure appears. Although it undoubtedly possesses a symbolic significance, its actual meaning is to this day a subject of controversy.

Its name is 'T'ao T'ieh', and it is a grotesque and crude mask with two big round eyes, but with the lower jaw missing. The large tusks rising from the upper jaw endow it with a ferocious and bestial appearance. From both sides of the nose sprout two inward-curving horns. A band usually runs under the eyes, rising upwards at right angles and ending in a tail. Under this band, on both sides of the jaw, crooked claws are visible. The most feasible theory concerning this mask is that it represents the head of a tiger with the lower jaw removed to enable a Shaman to slip it over his head for use in some unknown rite.

The etymology of the name 'T'ao T'ieh' is also uncertain: it appears unexpectedly in a few Chinese texts with a diversity of meanings. For example, in the *Chan hai king*, as translated by Legge and reported by Granet in his *Danses et Légendes*, it is a man-eating monster which lived on a mountain guarding rich copper mines.

These two forms—the Kuei and the T'ao T'ieh— are nearly always associated in such a way that the latter occupies a central position, while the two lateral Kuei appear as its continuation.

During the whole Shang period this representation (more rudimentary, of course, in the jade objects than in the bronzes) bears an expression of awe-inspiring ferocity. With advancing centuries this realism is mitigated and gradually superseded by more conventional stylisation. In the Pi's this kind of design is rather rare. In view of their annular shape, the decorative engravings for the most part display a continuous and regularly repeated pattern.

During the whole Western Chou period (in other words until the 7th century BC) the Shang style in carving shows a trend towards greater simplicity and becomes more primitive. Then follows the period historically known as that 'of the Springs and

1. Pi disc with large central hole, from the Royal Shang
Tombs, Hsiao T'un (Anyang). Academy of Arts, Honolulu.

2. Dagger or sacrificial knife. Middle Shang period.
Academy of Arts, Honolulu.

3. Point of a ceremonial lance, made of jade. Middle Shang period. Academy of Arts, Honolulu.

4. Ts'ung. Ritual symbol. Shang Yin period. Academy of Arts, Honolulu.

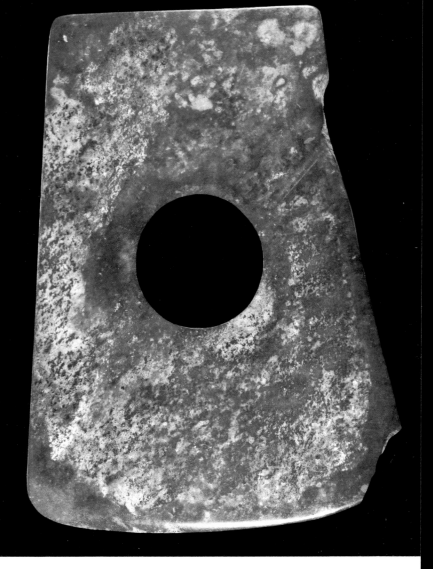

5. Pi disc in hatchet shape. Western Chou period. British Museum, London. Ex Eumorfopoulos Collection.

6. Strongly stylised human statuette. Late Chou or early Han period. British Museum, London. Ex Eumorfopoulos Collection.

7. Hilt of a short ceremonial sword. Middle Chou period.
Museo Nazionale Orientale, Rome. Fiacchi-Gisondi Collection.

8. Ts'ung. Ritual symbol. Probably Warring States. Victoria and Albert Museum, London.

9. Ts'ung. Ritual symbol. Middle Chou period. British Museum, London. Ex Eumorfopoulos Collection.

10. Basket-hilt of a short ceremonial sword. Warring States. Museo Nazionale Orientale, Rome. Fiacchi-Gisondi Collection.

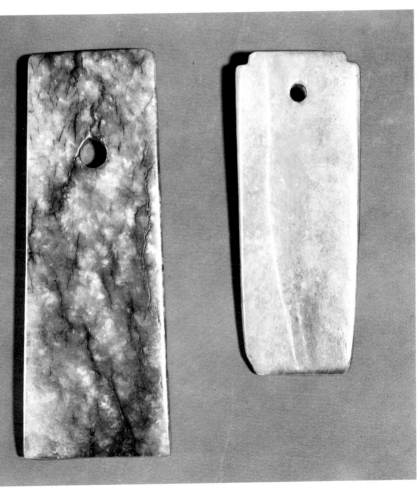

11 Chisels. Chou period. Museo Nazionale Orientale, Rome.
Fiacchi-Gisondi Collection.

12. Ritual Pi disc. Warring States. W. Rockhill Nelson
Gallery of Art, Kansas City.

13. Pendant in dragon shape. Late Chou period. Museo
Nazionale Orientale, Rome. Fiacchi-Gisondi Collection.

14. Ritual Pi disc. Warring States. W. Rockhill Nelson
Gallery of Art, Kansas City.

15. Pendant in stag shape. Late Chou period.
Metropolitan Museum, New York. Rogers Fund.

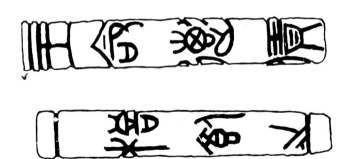

16. Ancient safe-conducts. Middle Chou period.

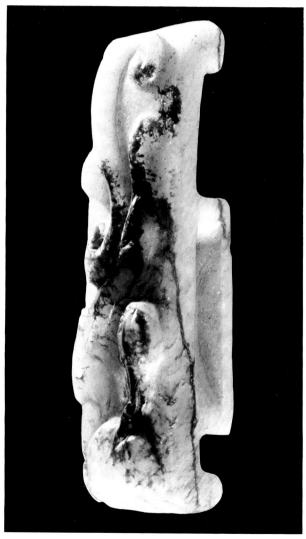

17. Sword-support for a belt. Warring States.
Museo Nazionale Orientale, Rome. Fiacchi-
Gisondi Collection.

Autumns' (771-481 BC), a name derived from the famous *Annals* of the Lu State, the country of Confucius. According to brief records referring to the time between the 6th and 4th centuries BC it was then that implements with corundum or diamond tips came into use, as can be deduced from the greater refinement of jade engravings. This new technique reaches its culmination in the following period (482-221 BC), known as the era 'of the Warring States' due to the fact that the central government suffered a complete loss of power, so that China was devastated by continuous wars between vassal states. Strangely enough, the continuous state of war did not seem to affect the development of arts, and particularly not the art of jade carving. Not only are the jade objects of this period superbly engraved, but also openwork carving of exquisite perfection first appears.

While keeping their basic shape and the traditional religious symbols, the Pi's of this period change from simple ring-shaped discs into objects of rare artistic beauty. In Plate 12 we can admire the specimen kept in the Nelson Gallery (Kansas City), which resembles closely the Pi originally belonging to the Imperial Treasure and presented by the Chinese Government at the First London Exhibition in 1935-1936. Made of the seldom found yellow nephrite, it gives a good idea of the artistic refinement attained towards the end of the Chou period. Incorporated into the outer edge of the disc are two perfectly carved imaginary monsters. The annular body, on the other hand, displays a precise geometrical pattern of tiny buttons—

which does not at first sight convey any idea of the exhausting work that went into carving this bas-relief out of jade that still presents a perfectly smooth and polished surface.

In my opinion this particular decorative pattern derives from the general concept of abundance and fertility, because these tiny protuberances can only represent grains of millet, the staple Chinese cereal of archaic times. Usually this kind of background decoration is called 'rice grain motif'; but such a definition seems erroneous because rice, now Asia's staple food, only reached China proper in comparatively recent times. In a predominantly agricultural civilisation the seed had probably assumed almost mystic significance, and the mystery of its transformation must have been associated with the religious Heaven-Earth dualism. As for the date of origin of the last-mentioned Pi, I should be inclined to conjecture the 5th-4th centuries BC.

A Pi in my own collection—which was found in a tomb of the Han period in southern Honan—appears at first sight completely dark brown and opaque. Holding it against the light, however, one discerns semi-transparent green areas whose colour is probably that of the original jade. And yet this state of deterioration and almost complete opacity cannot be taken as proof that the piece in question is of a more remote origin than the tomb itself. Its fairly well preserved geometrical decoration consists of small spirals which enclose a round protuberance. This is the more advanced symbol of fertility (in fact the seed and the germ that sprouts therefrom) which is found as a motif, both in carvings and in bronzes, as from the 3rd century BC and through the whole Han period.

This can be taken as a convincing demonstration of the fact that the degree of deterioration in jade is only a very general indication for determining its age. In fact, the rate of deterioration varies greatly according to the conditions of the place where the object has been preserved, and cannot therefore serve on its own as a basis for pinpointing its date. Among the various examples quoted in this book cases may be observed in which very ancient objects show far less marked deterioration than others of lesser age. The same principle, incidentally, applies to bronzes.

Among the jade in the Manlio Fiacchi collection, donated to the National Museum of Oriental Art in Rome but not yet exhibited or catalogued, I have found a curious specimen worthy of detailed description. This object, perhaps unique of its kind, reveals considerable progress in the technique of circular cutting roughly corresponding to that attained at the beginning of the Christian era; and in my opinion the specimen in question dates back to that period.

I am referring to an unfinished Pi on which the inner disc has been engraved but not entirely cut out. On the surface, where the cutting out process had been started with the aim of shaping the usual ring, there is an exactly circular groove several millimetres deep and with perfectly straight sides. It is obvious that it could not have been cut with a pointed bamboo stick or bone, for in that case the slanted cut of the pointed tip would have caused the sides of the groove to slope. And the exactitude of the circular outline seems to confirm the assumption that a most ingenious rotary apparatus was used. The theory seems justified that the craftsman in question had devised a kind of primitive vertical lathe consisting of a metal blade fixed longitudinally to a wooden pivot but gliding along a channel in such a way that hand pressure would keep it on the surface to be worked and allow the abrasive ointment to reach the friction point.

The other side of the jade disc is entirely covered with patterns similar to those on the Pi described before. One explanation is that a craftsman, instead of tracing out the central disc meant for cutting out and confining the ornaments to the outer ring, has proceeded to engrave the whole disc, as it is now. Then another worker probably saw only the smooth reverse side, on which he then started the usual cutting out operation. Halfway through it he must have looked at the other side to ascertain the depth of penetration and then noticed his error—whereupon he abandoned the work.

To finish this quick summary I should also like to mention a Pi made of white jade, with a serpentine pattern of interlacing lines which at first sight suggests the Warring States period. On closer examination, however, a certain 'softness' in the design becomes apparent, which points to a much later era. It is, in fact, almost certain that its date of origin is the reign of the Emperor Hui Tsung (1100-1126), a period characterised by a predilection for things ancient: hence the imitative nature of the design.

Seemingly a variation of the Pi is the 'Hsuan Chi'. I use the word 'seemingly' with good reason, because the latter—while still representing with its annular shape the curvature of the sky—was not only meant as a ritual symbol but had a definite practical use.

The Hsuan Chi consists of the usual disc with a large central hole, but its outer edge is marked by symmetrical indentations whose distance from each other alternates. Although its exact use is still subject to argument, it is generally considered an astronomical instrument. It seems that its purpose was to identify stars and determine the direction of the North Pole. No specimens have been found dating further back than the Shang period. Even so, it can be taken as a proof that the Chinese of more than three thousand years ago had some knowledge of astronomy.

According to one legend, the Emperor Fu Hsi (supposed to have reigned from 2852 to 2738 BC, although these dates derive more from traditional tales than from historical evidence) condemned to death two court astronomers because, by falling asleep one night, they failed in their duty of marking in the Imperial Annals the passing of a comet. The strange thing is that recent astronomical calculations confirm the passage of the comet in that period— though modern scholars reject the theory that the Emperor Fu Hsi ever really existed.

The Hsuan Chi started with a smooth surface, but was in later periods embellished with engraved lines and patterns which to this day lend themselves to widely differing interpretations.

Another typical jade object of symbolic character is the 'Ts'ung', a robust cylinder surrounded by a rectangular prism of square profile (Plate 8). The cylinder protrudes slightly at both ends of the prism. Each of the four sides has a central vertical rib, and parallel incisions of alternating depth link horizontally the rib and the edge of each side. The Ts'ung is the symbol of the Earth deity.

No specimen of this kind has been found in Neolithic tombs. This is no doubt due to the extreme difficulty of perforating a cylinder of such size, and of working a big block of particularly hard stone with the primitive tools of the times. The various specimens found in the Shang tombs were defined as jade by the Chinese and accepted as such by museums in the West. It is my opinion, however, that at least all those of the pre-Anyang period (and also the majority attributed to the Anyang period itself) are made not of jade but of a softer material which resembles marble.

The specimen which is now in the Honolulu Museum (Plate 4), and which has been reproduced from a photograph made on the Anyang excavation site, is probably the prototype of such objects carved in real jade. It is made of yellow nephrite with strongly marked reddish stains. Its rudimentary and somewhat coarse shape reveals the great difficulties that the ancient carver must have encountered. It has no indentations at the edges—these being a characteristic of all the other pieces found so far.

This fact discredits the theory of the probable origins of the Ts'ung advanced by Laufer. He starts from the notion that in the earliest ages the ancestral tablets of the monarchs, when not exhibited during ritual ceremonies, were kept in a tube protected by four slabs of jade which also had the purpose of preventing the tablets from rolling up. According to this theory the indentations at the edge of the square sides of a Ts'ung corresponded to the incisions made in the four rectangular tablets. This allowed a cord to be used to fix them in place, avoiding the risk of the cord slipping on the smooth cylinder. He does not contest the assumption that the Ts'ung represented the symbol of the Earth deity. The connection with the object's role as a receptacle for the archaic ancestral tablets had to be sought in the mythical origins of those reigning families which could be associated with the religious concept of Mother Earth.

Similar notions can be found in some Chinese texts which Laufer no doubt translated and consulted. There is no point in enumerating all the various theories which try to explain the origins and raison d'être of this object's shape. Although they are always based on ingenious arguments by logical deduction, they can be taken as no more than personal opinions.

One fairly plausible hypothesis, however, seems worth mentioning. Some authors maintain that, to start with, the object in question was simply a cylindrical tube and—in the primitive Chinese mud huts without windows—served as a kind of air-funnel or little chimney. Such an introduction of life-giving air and humidity might have been considered metaphorically as an essential link between heaven and earth. Still, no trace of such a cylindrical Ts'ung has been found so far in archaeological excavations.

It is fairly certain that, at first, these objects were comparatively tall. This fact does not in any way affect the theory of their function as receptacles for ancestral tablets, which anyway in the course of time tended to be squashed, almost to the point of becoming annular in shape during the Chou period. It is worth repeating, however, that most of the archaic tall Ts'ung are probably not made of genuine jade, even though the Chinese classify them as 'Yü'.

Let us pass from these objects of symbolic significance to implements more widely used—although in view of their great value they were in ancient times predominantly used only in ritual ceremonies. Here then is a summary description of some weapons and cutting implements made of jade.

Just because the use of such objects was the prerogative of the more cultured classes (mainly potentates and priests) they very often represent artistic achievement at its highest. In view of jade's high degree of hardness it is not surprising that before the discovery of metals it was accepted as the most suitable material for the blades of knives and daggers. This tradition persisted well into the Bronze Age.

Archaeological finds prove that during the whole 2nd millennium human sacrifices were part of the common rites performed at funerals of important persons. In some tombs of the Shang Dynasty, dozens of skeletons were found in the central burial chamber around the dead king or prince. In accordance with an unknown ritual their skulls were aligned separately, all turned in the same direction. In one of these tombs a heavy jade axe was found with two holes in the thick side. That is where the wooden handle was fixed, but by now it had disintegrated into dust. There is little doubt that this was a beheading axe.

In this period the priests possessed great religious and political power, often greater than that of the sovereign. Therein lies the explanation for the exquisite artistry of ancient sacrificial knives, which were in all probability used exclusively by priests. The blade was usually of jade, with a bronze hilt either carved or inlaid with such precious stones as turquoise or lapis lazuli. The mounting of the hard stones, done more than 3000 years ago, is so perfect that many a present-day goldsmith could learn from it. Similarly beautiful were the halberds, which were probably never used for combat but only for the lavish court ceremonial of the Shang or Chou Emperors. These specimens of rare magnificence, mostly found in the Anyang excavation zone, can be seen today in various museums. All this glory then began to fade with the advent of the Iron Age and the Han Dynasty (206 BC).

Little jade discs in various colours—either smooth or with patterns and with two or three holes meant for fixing to the apparel—were used by the Chinese in all ages, from the end of the 3rd millennium onwards. The simplest and most ancient form, which dates back to the Neolithic Age, is seen in a coarsely oval disc with three irregular holes at the long end. While the irregular shapes of the conical holes bear witness to the great difficulties experienced by the artisan in the carving process, the somewhat un-ambitious decoration can be taken as a proof that jade was chiefly appreciated for the magical qualities attributed to it, and that such beliefs already existed among the Chinese in the Neolithic era.

Many small jade objects, shaped in stylised animal forms, were found in the tombs of the Shang and the Chou dynasty. Making deductions from their formal and ornamental qualities it is possible to establish an approximate chronology of their origin. Thus fishes, crickets and owls, carved more or less coarsely from jade fragments, with no decoration whatever or with the engraving of a few simple geometrical lines, date back to the first Shang period. A more elaborate decoration, but still engraved lightly on objects of simple shape, is the usual sign pointing to the period between the 12th and the 7th centuries BC. In the late Chou period forms become more realistic and elaborate: frequently they represent stylised snakes and stag-like animals with ramified horns. Towards the end of the Chou period, between the 5th and the 3rd centuries, artistry in the carving of these ornaments reaches the peak of its perfection, as I pointed out before when speaking about the probable use of diamond and corundum-tipped tools in that era. Buttons, buckles, bracelets and innumerable accessories of clothing and coiffure are often absolute masterpieces as far as inventiveness and artistic achievement is concerned; and the size of the objects in question is mostly diminutive.

Together with the skeleton remnants found in the Shang and Chou tombs, numerous tiny jade objects were retrieved which had, however, a far from decorative function. They mainly consisted of small fragments of jade carved into the shape of crickets or into little cylinders only a few millimetres in diameter. The latter particularly are calcinated to such an extent that they have completely lost the look of jade. According to ancient texts they are objects associated with burial ceremonies and their use is rooted in an ancient superstition.

For the Chinese the concept of the soul has always been somewhat nebulous. The general belief was that at the moment of death the 'Superior Spirit' of an individual immediately fled the body in the direction of a not very well defined celestial limbo which was in a typically Chinese way described as the 'Yellow Sources'.

The official announcement of an Emperor's death, for instance, summed up the event thus: 'The Son of Heaven has descended to the Yellow Sources.'

Western commentators interpret this expression as descending into the Underworld. This seems fairly exact considering the Latin meaning of 'Inferos'—Kingdom of the Dead, or of the Souls. For the Chinese, however, the Paradise-Hell dualism in its traditional sense has never existed. In my opinion, therefore, this is an allusion to a mythical kingdom situated in the mountains where the Yellow River (Hoang Ho) starts. This stream has all through the ages been identified with China's protective deity, playing somewhat the same role as the Nile in the time of the Pharaohs.

But apart from this 'Superior' or 'Celestial' Spirit which left the body immediately at the moment of death, it was believed that various other 'earthly' spirits existed which for the time being stayed behind in the dead body. These had to be appeased with offerings and delicately enjoined to depart—which was accomplished by complicated rites which could extend over several months, particularly if the deceased was rich. In the interval there was a pious apprehension that they might become angry, leave the body and cause relatives serious troubles. It was to prevent these body spirits from getting at large before the end of the purification ceremonies (and perhaps also to prevent the body decaying) that the little jade objects were employed: the eyes and the mouth were covered with the tiny crickets, while the small cylinders were used to plug the body's natural openings. Besides, in a predominantly agricultural civilisation the cricket as a symbol of summer, and hence of ripening crops, must have possessed a mythical-religious significance, which explains the representation of the tiny insect all through the ages in innumerable decorative patterns.

Jade statuettes representing persons or animals are extremely rare before the Christian era. A figure of a crouching man—at present in a Chinese collection—is the only example of a carved human figure found in a Shang tomb. But in actual fact it has been carved out of a soft stone; similarly, the famous white tiger (also from the Shang period), mentioned in various records and in some of them described as jade, is made of a sort of marble. Both these art works were excavated in the Anyang zone, and therefore their origin can be pinpointed to the period between the 14th and 12th centuries BC.

A figure from the former Eumorfopoulos Collection (now in the British Museum), in green-grey nephritic jade with black and brown streaks, is usually accepted as dating back to the Chou period. Its attire, however, is characteristic of the first Han period, and personally I am convinced that its origin is not earlier than the 3rd to 2nd centuries BC.

From the same period, or a little later, came various water buffaloes (pre-eminently a beast of burden in the fertile Chinese plains) carved in the round out of blocks of jade. It is pretty obvious that jade carvers were as a rule inclined to represent animals in a lying position, with legs bent towards the belly, for the simple reason that with a particularly hard material the representation of a standing animal offered considerably greater difficulties. No reason, however, has been found to explain why in every case the head of the beast is turned outwards and its mouth half-open in a near-grin—as if they had been conceived by a contemporary Walt Disney.

The horse's head reproduced in this book (Plate 22), made of spotless green jade of excellent quality, belongs no doubt to the end of the Han period; that is, it cannot be earlier than the 2nd century AD. This conclusion is based on its bowed head and the fact that the figure—although stylised and carved in the round—lacks that vigour and fierceness which are characteristic of analogous sculptures discovered in tombs of the period between the 2nd century BC and the beginning of the first Christian century.

Until and all through the T'ang period (618-906) statuary in human form in jade appears practically non-existent, perhaps because of the splendid superiority of the art of clay-moulding. In fact jade sculpture could hardly compete with the perfect moulding and the subtlety of detail so much appreciated nowadays in ancient terracotta statuettes. Even so, there are various little reproductions of animals dating back to T'ang times, and they already reveal a remarkable sense of realistic proportions.

There is one everyday object that has played its part in the life of the average Chinese for 4000 years, and still does. It is his personal seal. It is no secret that until the comparatively recent past the vast majority of the Chinese were unable to write. Knowledge of their particularly difficult writing was confined to a small class of lettered men. As a result it was normal practice to have public letter-writers: sometimes scholars who had fallen into disgrace, sometimes those who had failed to pass their higher examinations. Hence the necessity to authenticate the letters or commercial agreements written by such scribes.

The seal was recognised absolutely and honoured everywhere like a personal signature. That of the monarch was the very symbol of power. In Chinese history, full as it is of palace revolutions, sometimes culminating in the reigning monarch's assassination, there is frequent mention of the care taken to hide or steal the imperial signet, since in its absence a successor might have some difficulty in being recognised as legitimate.

Wealthy people usually possessed a seal made of jade because it was indestructible and impossible to alter. Examples range from a simple oval plaque with a hole designed for a string with which to tie the signet to the belt, to an enormous massive square (weighing sometimes several pounds) as evolved in more recent times. These larger and more solid seals are often artfully engraved or carved on one side, while the smooth inscription side often bears not only the name of the owner but also all his titles, public offices, etc.

The appearance of the engraved letters on these seals does not contradict my earlier statement that inscriptions on jade objects begin only in the 18th century on account of the insuperable difficulty of engraving small characters with primitive metal tools.

On the seals the letters are always big and of a kind that hardly requires special technical skill. In fact they can be engraved even on a material as hard as jade without the use of diamond or corundum tips.

There are two more typically Chinese objects which are nearly always made of jade: they are the 'Kuei' and the 'Ju I'.

The Kuei is an elongated tablet, never wider than about two inches, so that it can easily be held in the palm of the hand. It is at one and the same time a kind of baton of command and a sort of visiting card containing the name, functions and possibly the special merits of a person. To an artist his Kuei could be a present from the monarch in recognition of his high merits; to a court official called to service, a kind of Marshal's baton.

The Ju I is a strange kind of elegantly curved sceptre. It was used on solemn occasions (receptions, etc.) not only by the sovereign but also by dignitaries of great wealth. Seated, the gracious host would receive the compliments of his guests, clutching the Ju I in his right hand. Or, if he was a judge, he would pronounce verdicts in court in the same position. This sceptre was also used sometimes as a special gift, sent to somebody as a sign of respect and high esteem.

Plate 16 shows something of a curiosity—the design, copied from the original many years ago, of two strange objects which could easily be taken for two Kuei but are something completely different. The originals are not accessible, and it may be that

18. Hilt of a ceremonial sword. Warring States. Museo
Nazionale Orientale, Rome. Fiacchi-Gisondi Collection.

19 Ritual Pi disc. Warring States. Museo Nazionale
Orientale, Rome. Fiacchi-Gisondi Collection.

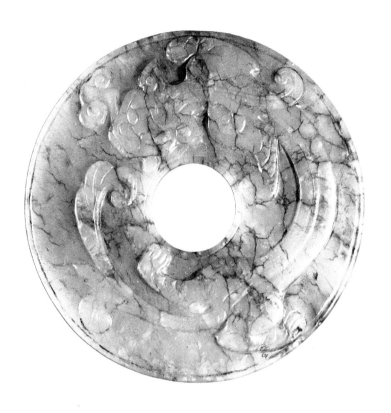

20. Ritual Pi disc. Warring States. Museo Nazionale
Orientale, Rome. Fiacchi-Gisondi Collection.

21. Stylised tiger, sculptured all round. Han period. Museo Poldi Pezzoli, Milan.

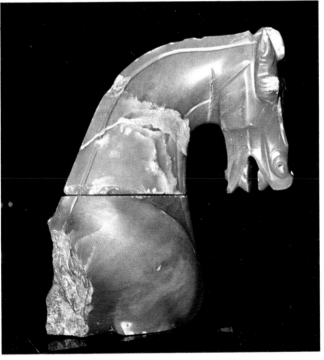

22. Horse's head. Han period. Victoria and Albert Museum, London.

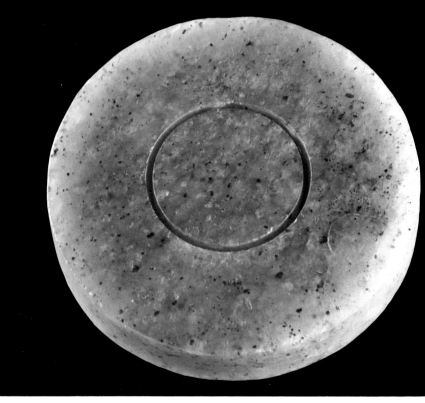

23. Disc in greenish-white jade, with black dots. Han period.
Museo Nazionale Orientale, Rome. Fiacchi-Gisondi
Collection.

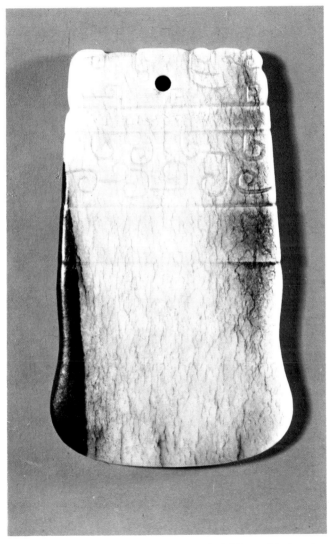

24. Pendant in hatchet shape. Han period. Museo Nazionale Orientale, Rome. Fiacchi-Gisondi Collection.

25. Double belt-buckle. Han period. Private Collection, Milan. Ex Fiacchi-Gisondi Collection.

26. Ritual Pi disc. Han period. Museo Nazionale Orientale,
Rome. Fiacchi-Gisondi Collection.

27. Pendant: serpent-like dragon. Probably Sung period.
British Museum, London.

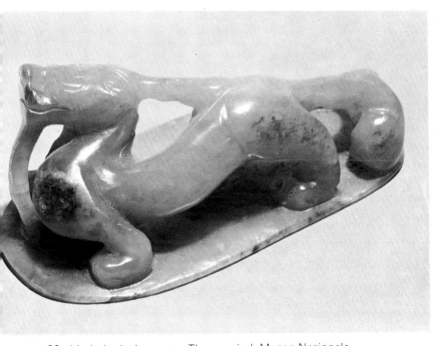

28. Mythological monster. T'ang period. Museo Nazionale
Orientale, Rome. Fiacchi-Gisondi Collection.

29. Duck or other bird. T'ang period. British Museum, London. Ex Eumorfopoulos Collection.

30. Duck, carved in the round. T'ang period. Museo Poldi Pezzoli, Milan.

31. Goat-like animal. T'ang period. Museo Nazionale
Orientale, Rome. Fiacchi-Gisondi Collection.

32. Crouching animal. T'ang period. Museo Poldi Pezzoli, Milan.

34. Pendant in small hatchet shape. Sung period. Museo
Nazionale Orientale, Rome. Fiacchi-Gisondi Collection.

Goblet for festive occasions. Sung period. Victoria and
bert Museum, London.

35. Cylindrical bracelet. Sung period. Museo Nazionale
Orientale, Rome. Fiacchi-Gisondi Collection.

36. Pendant with mythological animals. Sung period. Museo
Nazionale Orientale, Rome. Fiacchi-Gisondi Collection.

37. Cylindrical receptacle for washing paint-brushes. Sung period. Museo Poldi Pezzoli, Milan.

38. Bowl. Sung period. Museo Poldi Pezzoli, Milan.

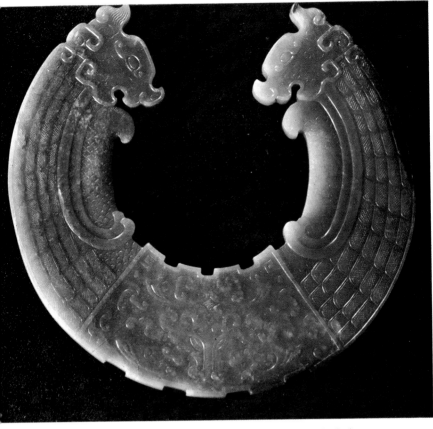

39. Crescent-shaped plaque. Sung period. Musée Guimet, Paris.

40. Mythical monster, sculptured all round. Probably late Sung. Museo Poldi Pezzoli, Milan.

41. Receptacle in shape of ritual archaic bronze (Kuei).
Yüan or early Ming period. Academy of Arts, Honolulu.

42. Bowl. Ming period. British Museum, London. Ex Eumorfopoulos Collection.

43. Big tortoise. Ming period. British Museum, London.

44. Cicada-shaped pendant. Ming period. Museo Nazionale
Orientale, Rome. Fiacchi-Gisondi Collection.

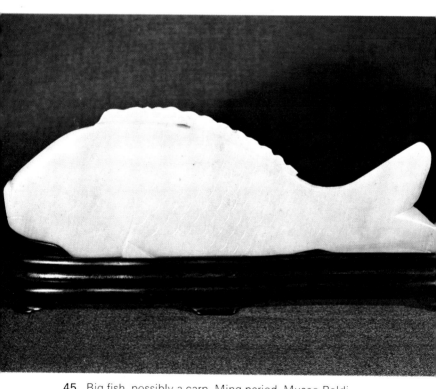

45. Big fish, possibly a carp. Ming period. Museo Poldi
Pezzoli, Milan.

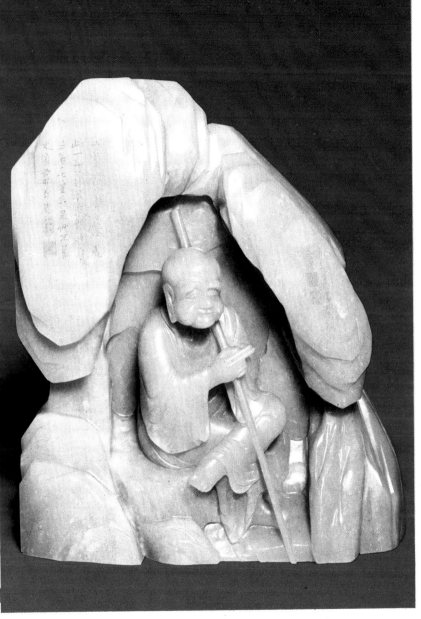

46. An Immortal meditating in a grotto. Ming period.
Metropolitan Museum, New York.

47. Pendant in sounding-stone shape. Ch'ing period. Museo
Nazionale Orientale, Rome. Fiacchi-Gisondi Collection.

48. Bowl. Ch'ing period. Victoria and Albert Museum, London.

49. Belt buckle. Ch'ing period. Museo Nazionale
Orientale, Rome. Fiacchi-Gisondi Collection.

the archaic characters are not very well drawn. The truth is that these ancient pieces were calcified and damaged to such an extent that the inscription was hardly visible at all.

Actually these two jades are possibly the prototypes of the very first passports. They are safe-conducts: one for river journeys, and one to tell the guards to admit the bearer to a not clearly specified city. I was told that they both dated back to the reign of Suen Wang of the Chou Dynasty (827-781 BC). Both are made of a brownish jade which is opaque and considerably decayed.

Such objects as cups and bowls made of jade are chronologically among the latest examples of Chinese carving art. This can be explained quite satisfactorily. It is easy to imagine what a hard task it must have been to cut a jade block in two halves and then to transform each into a bowl-shaped vessel without the help of modern rotary implements. The first such vessels, produced towards the end of the Chou period (if one is to believe the doubtful dates accepted by some museums), as well as those of the following centuries (throughout the T'ang period) are all thick-walled. Although many ancient poems extol the thinness of the wine goblets and tea cups made of genuine jade and used amidst the splendour of the Imperial court of the T'ang period, no such specimens have so far been discovered anywhere.

Actually, it is likely that in the descriptions of ancient ballads the fine clay cups ('Yüeh') from Cheking, with their grey-green or greenish-blue colour have been confused with genuine jade. So, for instance, we read in a famous ancient poem: 'The Yüeh cups of splendid jade colour made the tea look red...'

Both logical deduction and written evidence found in ancient records point to the nature of the machine used for the cutting in half of the jade blocks—which were certainly of boulder shape, since the material in question (used until the 12th century AD) was certainly of alluvial origin. In order to make round or oval bowls, a round iron disc was probably used (called in Chinese 'cha t'o'), centrally fitted on to a straight, long wooden stick; the latter was rotated by means of a wooden mechanism consisting of a pulley, a connecting rod and a pedal. Since, however, the technique of using iron was at its beginnings halfway through the Chou period, and remained in a rudimentary stage until the end of that period, it is hardly imaginable that such a contraption came into use before the Christian era.

Many authors seem to interpret too literally the information contained in ancient texts when they refer to jade goblets, vases and other receptacles being used not only at the courts of the Chou Dynasty but even at those of Shang rulers. In the first place one has to remember the confusion deriving from the indiscriminate use of the word 'Yü' which, as previously explained, had more than one meaning, embracing a range of minerals other than genuine jade and of varying hardness. Second, it is quite possible that the receptacles referred to were not made of jade but were simply decorated with jade. This is quite feasible because bronze manufacture was highly developed from Shang times, and it was current practice to embellish bronzes with inlaid stones, including jade.

There is no doubt that stone vessels of the same shape and style as the ritual bronzes were produced in the Shang and Chou periods. Many of them have been excavated in the Anyang zone, but even a superficial scrutiny clearly shows that they have been carved rather coarsely out of a soft marble-like material. Instead of being objects of high value, they were at the time only modest substitutes for bronzes — all the more so since the use of this metal was then a privilege of the rich and powerful. From the Sung period the fashion of imitating archaic objects and ornaments became widespread and has survived to our own times. That is why it is often very difficult to establish the age of a jade object, even if it dates back only a few centuries, being, that is, produced at a time when tools and abrasives invented in the Western world were unknown in China.

In the Freer Art Gallery in Washington there are two bowls, one oval and the other heart-shaped (perhaps for reasons of economy and the craftsman's desire to follow the shape of the original jade block and thus to use the precious material to the maximum). They are comparatively thin at the edges but lower down the walls thicken. On the outside they display an engraved geometrical pattern. They are classified as originating from the 4th-3rd centuries BC, and if this theory is correct they are certainly exceptional.

In my opinion, jade cups and bowls boasting really fine walls cannot have been produced before the end of the 17th century.

THE EVOLUTION OF JADE-CARVING TECHNIQUE

The invention of the wooden foot-lathe dates back to the period preceding Christ's birth, and that of the rotating iron disc—designed, according to authoritative ancient texts, to cut to size and halve jade blocks—to the period of Six Dynasties (AD 265-589). During the centuries that followed only very slight progress was made in the technique of jade-carving.

It could almost be said that the only innovation introduced concerned variations in the use of the abrasive powders. The substance first used for this purpose was quartz-containing sand (hardness 7) which had the advantage of being found in nature ready-made. The next stage of development brought pulverised garnets (hardness 7·5) into use. There are in China vast deposits of these crystals, which are slightly harder than quartz. After the first crushing process, accomplished in huge mortars, the method adopted to obtain extremely fine powder was not unlike that used to produce oil from olives in southern Italy.

A sturdy iron pivot was fixed vertically in the centre of a flat round stone. On to the pivot was slipped a short wooden beam with a hole of such size that it could rotate easily. Solidly wedged in the centre of this beam (in a horizontal position) was another big iron pivot designed to receive a heavy stone cylinder of such diameter as would allow it to rest freely on the base on which the material to be pulverised would be deposited. A donkey harnessed to the end of the wooden beam was made to walk round and round, thus keeping the machinery in motion. The powder was then collected and strained through an extremely fine sieve. The larger particles which did not pass through the sieve were once more put through the mill.

In about the 13th century an even more efficient abrasive came into use: pulverised corundum, known under the name of 'black sand'. Strangely enough, the garnet powder was called 'red sand', although its colour is off-white.

In the 13th century, towards the end of the Sung Dynasty, new interest in the art of jade-carving was stimulated by the arrival in China of big jade boulders from the quarries of Turkestan, and this led to an increased demand for the abrasives. Contemporary records still in existence show that the Mongol conqueror Kublai Khan charged some public servants with making a survey of all the deposits of these abrasives. When fixing the tributes due to the court annually from the various provinces, he also in some cases apportioned a certain quantity of these abrasive materials as part of the tribute.

It is certain that the Yüan were responsible for the

production of some jade objects of enormous size. Apart from confirmation found in written records, the actual proof of this lies in the existence of some specimens which could not be removed because of their immense weight. The most famous of these is the 'Wine Bowl' (although this Chinese description is perhaps misleading) on which in the first years of the 14th century Brother Odorico da Pordenone reported in detail, mentioning that it was 'two paces high'. According to this missionary (the first to visit China) the vessel stood in a courtyard in the centre of Kublai Khan's Imperial Palace in Peking and was filled with rice wine on the occasion of great banquets. The guests then drew wine from it with golden goblets. In his description of this unique urn he speaks of its magnificent decorations of gold and pearls.

The existence of this exceptional vessel, which must have been carved out of an enormous jade boulder weighing several tons, is incontestable. Its description, however, may be slightly exaggerated and the assertion regarding its use is perhaps erroneous. The fact is that such vessels were, as a rule, used by the Chinese as goldfish bowls, since in those times they delighted in keeping and admiring these little creatures. Also, my long experience of life in China has taught me that the Chinese have always preferred their wine warmed up, not cold—and it is difficult to imagine how they could keep the drink at the temperature required in such a huge jade receptacle.

As a matter of fact, it is improbable that Odorico

da Pordenone ever had access to the interior of the Imperial Palace, and it is even less likely that he was present at a banquet. He might have had his information from some palace official, who is likely to have embellished it in the habitual manner. Still, the essential particulars are confirmed in trustworthy records of the time.

It is obvious that the carving and engraving of objects of such size not only took years of hard work but also necessitated enormous quantities of abrasive. Thus it seems that the deposits of the precious 'black sand', extensively used by the Yüan, gave out somewhere around the beginning of the Ming period (AD 1368).

Books of the 15th and 16th centuries mention exclusively the 'red sand', that is, the powder made of pulverised garnets. Still, during the Ming period also, jade objects of considerable size were produced —although, as a rule, not in the shape of bowls and vases. The big tortoise in the British Museum (reproduced here in Plate 43) is about two feet long. If the dragon, incidentally, ranks highest as the symbol of royalty and of China herself, the tortoise follows closely in symbolic importance by reason of its shape. For the Chinese, the curved back represented the vault of Heaven and the flat belly the Earth. Thus the simple animal shape in a way symbolised the whole universe.

With the advent of the Ch'ing, the last of the Imperial Dynasties (1644-1911), jade-carving received a new and potent stimulus. Currently the quantities of nephrite arriving from Turkestan were increasing, and about the middle of the 18th century the imports of jadeite from Burma into China started, soon to be followed by the appearance of Siberian jade. Also new sources of corundum were discovered in Chinese territory, and the manufacture of the precious abrasive, as well as the technique of its utilisation, was perfected.

Instead of using pure corundum powder on a basis of grease, Chinese lapidaries began to experiment with various mixtures of which each family jealously guarded the secret. As a rule they consisted in a combination of corundum and very fine clay, with possible additions of quartz and garnets, which were always ground to an exceedingly fine texture. These compounds, in use up to this day, require only the addition of some water to form a semi-liquid batter.

This new method had several advantages. In the first place, it offered the possibility of using an un-skilled servant, or even a child, in the working process. Such a person had only to drop the abrasive in a continuous trickle from a bowl held above the surface being worked. At the same time this reduced the heat produced by the friction of the carving process. Moreover, the use of a newly invented big saw for cutting large blocks became possible, whereas the old-fashioned iron disc could never be made in a large size. This new tool, called by the Chinese a 'four-band saw', consisted originally of a fine iron wire kept taut by a robust bow. Two workmen seated on two sides of the boulder sawed, maintaining a regular see-saw motion, while a third made the abrasive mixture drip from above; it was collected in a basin underneath and kept for repeated use. This system eliminated also the fumes and odours of over-heated grease which had been caused by friction.

Among experts the assertion is common that the golden age of jade-carving was in the 18th century, during the reign of the Emperor Ch'ien Lung (1736-1795). I do not entirely agree with such statements. In fact, technical accomplishment in this field reached its zenith under the rule of K'ang Hsi (1662-1722), when the diamond tip came into use and consequently the quality of the engravings became most exquisite. Unfortunately it is extremely difficult to distinguish between the jades of these two periods, and a mere technicality makes this task even harder: while many pieces of the Ch'ien Lung period bear the unmis-takeable sign of the period, this is very rarely the case with the objects produced under K'ang Hsi. This absence of distinguishing marks is partly due to an ill-advised edict issued by a minister in 1676. It banned the use of the Imperial 'nien yao' on all fragile objects because the breaking of such objects would mean a grave offence against the Emperor's sacred name. Originally this order concerned only porcelain, but gradually it was extended also to jade.

At this point a brief digression may be useful to clear up the connection between a date and an Emperor's name. The Chinese calendar starts with the sixtieth year of the reign of the legendary Emperor Huang Ti, in 2637 BC. This date is traditionally accepted, although it is not strictly historical. From that year the count of time is based on cycles of 60 years each. Every year, instead of a numerical indication, bears a name formed by the combination of two characters: a celestial one and an earthly one (the name of an animal). Hence one finds in Chinese books references to 'Year of the Dog', 'Year of the Pig', 'Year of the Hare', and so on. These names are immutable and follow each other in the same order within every cycle. Thus, after pinpointing a year's chronological position within a cycle, one largely relies on guesswork in order to identify the cycle concerned; and indications in this respect are mostly scarce and vague. From an early period of Chinese history there was a tendency to eliminate this uncertainty when indicating a date in inscriptions, and to indicate instead the number of years which had elapsed since the monarch's accession to the throne. The Emperor dropped his original name at the beginning of his reign in order to assume a new one—coined by himself—which had to characterise both his personality and the period of his reign. This dynastic name, containing as a rule an augural formula, is called in Chinese 'nien yao'.

In connection with the problem of distinguishing the K'ang Hsi jades from those of the Ch'ien Lung period it may be as well to mention that in the former period not many of those highly complicated engravings were produced which reflect superb craftsmanship rather than true artistic quality. At that time the principal aim seemed to consist in good-quality material and simple classical form.

Moreover, when the stone under scrutiny turns out to be jadeite, we can be almost certain that the object was produced in the second half of the 18th century, because all through the 17th century only very small quantities of that stone reached China. Its massive import in quantity dates from the period that followed the peace treaty signed between the Emperor Ch'ien Lung and the government of Burma in 1784. The same applies to Siberian jade, which is dark green and speckled with black dots. It is otherwise very difficult to make definite statements where no certainty exists as to the origin of an object, because in dubious cases personal conviction or individual sensitivity may influence judgment. These views were also expressed by the High Commission of Chinese experts when in 1935 chosen pieces from the former Imperial Treasure, including some jade, were presented at the First London Exhibition.

During the long reign of Emperor Ch'ien Lung, the last great monarch of China (although his own origin was Manchu rather than Chinese), jade articles became fashionable to the point of veritable obsession.

Buddhism infiltrated into China in the first centuries of the Christian era and from the 5th or 6th century led to an impressive development of sculpture. And yet the wide range of pantheistic jade statuettes deriving from this religion dates back only to the 13th century. Very popular indeed in the West are the elegant feminine statuettes generally known under the Chinese name of 'Kuan Yin'. Very few people, however, are aware of the fact that in reality they represent the asexual reincarnation of the Future Buddha Avalokitesvara (i.e. the Compassionate).

In China this Bodhisattva assumed its indubitably feminine aspect at the beginning of the T'ang period (AD 618) and was then worshipped as a benevolent goddess, protectress of the crops and of women in labour. The Jesuits in their wisdom tried to integrate this Kuan Yin cult with that of the Madonna. As a result, the representation of this original Bodhisattva appears after AD 1700 frequently transformed into a statuette of a gracious female with a child in her arms, though more often in ceramic than in jade. Statuettes representing other Bodhisattvas are also comparatively common, for example Manjusri seated on a lion, and Samantabhadra riding an elephant. And for the Tao cult believers there were, of course, figures of Lao Tz'u and his Eight Immortals in the first place, plus all the symbolic animals associated with them, the bat, the stork and the gazelle, to mention but the most important.

In the 17th century snuff became popular in China, and consequently, 'snuff bottles' appeared—tiny jade flagons (usually oval) or flagons with a jade stopper equipped with a tiny spoon with which to scoop out the small quantities of pulverised tobacco as required.

There was practically no citizen in the capital who would not have at least a decorative jade button adorning his dress or hat. Wealthy people had richly engraved belt buckles made of jade or ornaments for the hair—which were not confined to the fair sex.

Table accessories in jade were popular with artists and men of letters: a cylinder for paint brushes, for instance, and brush supports on which to leave the writing brush momentarily while meditating. Further examples include little shades designed to reduce the glare of strong light and receptacles in which to dilute ink, which was made from tablets of hardened soot.

Very special sculptured representations that enjoyed great favour at the court of the Emperor Ch'ien Lung are known as 'jade mountains', and during his reign they could be seen almost everywhere in his vast palace. Some of these remarkable pieces weighed several hundred pounds. The monarch, himself an eminent artist and writer, took great pleasure in composing poems and writing them down with the paint brush; later they would be engraved with a diamond tip on the walls of these 'mountains' in an artful facsimile of his own handwriting. In fact, there are lines in these poems containing such sentiments as 'These words I have engraved on this exquisite, shining wall ...'

These 'mountains' are clearly inspired by the Tao cult; they represent famous summits, particularly the K'un Lun, associated with this religion. (This in spite of the fact that the official religion was in essence Buddhist. For to Chinese people religion has always been something abstract and vague; in some ceremonies both monks of the Buddha and the Tao cult took part, performing the rites separately, each according to his creed.)

Generally speaking, these 'mountains' consist of

huge monolithic boulders, with several peaks jutting out which are supposed to be the summits of a mountain chain. From the side walls little grottoes or shrines are carved out, peopled by human figures which represent the Immortals. The etymology of their Chinese name 'Hsien' is based on the two characters: 'Shan' (mountain) and 'Jen' (man).

Finally, thin jade slabs were used by the Chinese as a musical instrument. In place of bell-towers, which have never been known in China, many temples used to have slabs of jade hanging on cords and functioning as chimes. Striking them rhythmically in turn, a temple servant produced subdued and melodious sounds. Sometimes smaller and thinner pieces of jade were strung up on the outside of a temple, hanging on parallel strings very near to each other. The slightest puff of wind would make them tinkle and vibrate, producing sweet music.

In 1911 (with the advent of the Republic), or perhaps a little later, electric motors for the lathes reached China together with modern tools and carborundum grindstones. Thus, jade carving changed from an intricate art requiring infinite patience and skill into a fairly unexciting handicraft. Even for a layman it is not too difficult to tell the difference between an ancient jade piece and a modern one. The mechanically driven grindstones with their high abrasive potential produce clear and hard-cutting surfaces which were impossible to attain with the ancient methods. What is even more important, the nephritic jade polished with modern high-speed rotating discs presents a coldly smooth surface but lacks the exquisitely subdued shine of the ancient pieces.

Moreover, whenever mechanical methods replace manual work, the stamp of human personality disappears, together with all those tiny imperfections which endow the finished work with vibrant life. There is no longer any trace of the alert mind that inspires the hand with the passionate urge to create beauty . . . The work itself may be more perfect, it is true, but it will always have a certain coldness; it no longer speaks straight to the heart.

JADE IN PRE-COLUMBIAN AMERICA

In the vast area that encompasses the southern part of North America, Central America and the northern part of South America many civilisations succeeded each other over the ages and superimposed their characteristics on each other. For the sake of simplicity and because of ethnic and artistic analogies I propose to use the term 'Central America' for the whole area which surrounds the Gulf of Mexico. The area of the Maya culture extends from Mexico to the Yucatan Peninsula. The beginnings of this civilisation probably date back to the 3rd millennium, but no archaeological evidence whatsoever is available from that period. The first historical document which can be dated with certainty is an engraved slab of nephritic jade of the 2nd century AD. From that time onwards the Maya began erecting a commemorative stele every twenty years.

A marvellous funeral mask is exhibited in the Mexico City Museum. Made of jade, it has powerfully sculptured features of exceptional expressive force. It was found in a crypt near the village of S. Domingo, in the Mexican state of Chiapas, and can be pinpointed to the 5th or 6th century AD, which is the golden age of Maya art.

Strangely enough, after another three or four centuries this civilisation seems to have worn itself out. The reasons for this loss of strength seem all the more inexplicable as today there are still several million people who must be the direct descendants of the Maya. Of course, most of them exist in utterly miserable conditions.

In the Gulf of Mexico three main civilisations have succeeded each other, the first of them—Olmec—being by far the most important. Archaeology has given us the fullest evidence of an impressive jade-carving art which flourished there between the 5th and the 1st centuries BC. The raw material used is not actually genuine nephrite in most cases, but jadeite. Although the workmanship of these jade carvers never reached the heights of contemporary Chinese artistry, it shows unusual skill combined with remarkable artistic sensitivity. This deeply human sensitivity derived partly, perhaps, from the fact that all the work was done by hand, without any knowledge of iron and without the help of any of the ingenious rotary tools invented by the Chinese. The

50. Bowl with lid. Ch'ing period. Victoria and Albert Museum,
London.

51. Hsi Wang Mu accompanied by a phoenix. Ch'ing period.
Victoria and Albert Museum, London.

52. Small group of personages. Ch'ing period. Victoria and
Álbert Museum, London. W. H. Cape legacy.

53. Sculptured panel: the Immortals in a retreat. Ch'ing period.
Victoria and Albert Museum, London. Wells legacy.

54. Medallion or garment button. Ch'ing period. Victoria and Albert Museum, London. Wells legacy.

55. Round jade medallion. Ch'ing period. Victoria and Albert Museum, London.

56. Sauce-boat in shape of archaic bronze. Ch'ing period.
Museo Poldi Pezzoli, Milan.

57. Two ceremonial sceptres (Ju I). Ch'ing period. Museo Nazionale Orientale, Rome. Fiacchi-Gisondi Collection.

58. Jar with lid marked Ch'ien Lung. Ch'ing period. Museo Poldi Pezzoli, Milan.

59. Sculptured plaque representing a deity. Maya art.
American Museum of Natural History, New York.

60. Statuette of seated man. Maya art. Museo Nacional de
Antropología, Mexico City.

61. Human mask in mosaic made of jade fragments. Maya art. Museo Nacional de Antropología, Mexico City.

62. Breast-plate worn at ritual ceremonies. Zapotec civilisation. Museo Nacional de Antropología, Mexico City.

63. Statuette of 'dragon', sculptured all round. Olmec art. American Museum of Natural History, New York.

64. Statuette of weeping child, sculptured all round. Olmec art. Museo Nacional de Antropología, Mexico City.

65. Hei-tiki amulet. Maori art. Museo Pigorini, Rome.

only metals known then were gold and copper. Obviously, the former was too soft to be suitable, and the second too scarce to be used by craftsmen. The only tools employed in shaping the jadeite were probably pieces of obsidian or volcanic lava. The objects excavated from the Maya's ancient dwellings or tombs are mostly statuettes and pendants representing humans, either erect or squatting. The oldest are carved in the round, with an accentuated stylisation of the features. In its peak period, however (3rd to 1st centuries BC), Olmec art presents also details of almost anatomical exactitude.

In the northern region of Vera Cruz a Totonac civilisation developed between the 4th and the 10th centuries AD. Their gem cutting art was of a high standard, but among the excavations jade objects are rather scarce. Those found might not even have been produced locally, and the raw material must at any rate have been imported. The minerals mainly used were diorite and various types of soft marble.

The Huastec civilisation came into being to the north of the preceding Totonac. It has left vestiges of a well developed art of clay moulding and characteristic pottery, but the gem cutting art is hardly worth mentioning.

On the Mexican plateau various civilisations followed each other after the Neolithic Age, but little is known about them, and they left hardly any artistic heritage. Towards the beginning of the Christian era, however, a civilisation appeared which was to flourish for ten centuries and has left a great number of imperishable works of art.

It is somewhat strange that the original name of the people responsible for this civilisation is not known to us. Historically the name Teotihuacán is accepted, but it is fairly certain that this is the name given by the Aztecs to an important city situated where the great Sun Pyramid stands, this colossal structure having been built towards the middle of the 1st millennium by the original inhabitants of the region called Teotihuacán. It is beyond the scope of this work to deal with this superb monument and the artistic activities of its builders. It is, however, worth mentioning that they excelled in one form of art: their funeral masks, carved in jade or porphyry, are remarkably naturalistic and expressive.

In the 10th century this race was overcome by the Toltec, and the following period is to a certain extent characterised by the ornamental motifs preponderant in jade sculpture. Human form gives way to shapes inspired by the animal kingdom: mostly jaguars and winged serpents.

The Aztec descended from the north towards the end of the 13th or the beginning of the 14th century; then their penetration of the Mexican tableland commenced. In about 1330 they founded their capital, Tenochtitlan, where Mexico City stands today.

They swiftly came to dominate all the neighbouring tribes towards whom, however, they displayed great tolerance: instead of destroying the defeated, they rather absorbed them. This mixture of races and cultures gave rise to a magnificent civilisation which unfortunately lasted only about two centuries before being destroyed by Cortez and his followers.

Aztec jade carving art derives directly from the art of the Toltec and Olmec. Statuettes of deities, sculptured in jadeite, are frequent. They mostly look solemn and hieratic, and their identity is often obscure. Representations of the jaguar and the winged or feathered serpent, typical of the Toltec art, occur again in the same style.

This feathered serpent is obviously of totemistic origin. It was at first simply a stylised symbol but became in course of time the very emblem of a powerful deity. The feathers with which it is adorned must be considered a royal attribute. This reverential cult may be partly due to the abundance of deadly snakes in the region concerned, but there is another possible reason. Only the sovereign or the High Priest could decree death. Therefore beasts like the jaguar or the snake—which could kill without the slightest warning—became the object of reverence.

The animal representations engraved or sculptured in jade by Aztec artists are of exceptional naturalistic artistry. Skulls, either single or in chains, are also a frequently used ornamental motif, which is not surprising in view of the practice of propitiatory human sacrifices.

Interesting jadeite statuettes or pendants inspired by the human form have also been found in Costa Rica, but their symbolic significance more often than not escapes our understanding and becomes an object of controversy. Their style mostly bears the mark of a hieratic stylisation which possesses an individual and strange fascination.

Some descendants of the original population still exist in the northern region of the Amazon River, in glades carved out of impenetrable and awesome forest; their ancestors took refuge there from the onslaught of Brazil's Portuguese conquerors. There are only a few tribes—the Chavante, the Jivaro, etc.— counting now no more than several thousand people, whose development is still in the Paleolithic phase. Protected by the natural hazards of their forbidding surroundings, they avoid any contact with the outside world. Thus the limited information available concerning their existence and customs can generally be gleaned only from the few brave missionaries who withstand the perils of a deadly climate and live totally isolated in this enormous area several times the size of Great Britain.

Some years ago in Rio de Janeiro I received for the first time information about the jade amulets worn by some tribes of Indians. It was an Italian missionary, on his way back home after ten years in Equatorial Amazonia, who told me that he saw one of these amulets attached to a string and hanging round the neck of a Jivaro chief. He described it as a small green pebble, coarsely shaped like a human head and without any artistic pretensions. Having acted as a doctor and cured this chief when he was gravely ill, the missionary had been on particularly friendly terms with him. Despite this, an attempt to acquire the amulet in question caused considerable animosity, which persisted for some time and was only dispelled with difficulty.

As things are—with one-third of the Amazon area still unexplored territory—it is impossible to ascertain whether there exist any alluvial deposits of jade or jadeite there. There are, it is true, some adventurers who in defiance of all perils search for precious stones in the riverbeds of those innumerable 'igarapés' (small rivulets with changeable courses) which form an inextricable maze in the midst of the equatorial forests. But they, even if the expedition has been successful, are hardly inclined to reveal details of their activities for fear of taxes and official interference. (Brazil is the second greatest diamond producing country in the world, but according to government estimates 98 per cent of these precious stones are simply smuggled out of Brazil.)

It is also conceivable that any jade pieces found in the Amazon region (and there are only vague reports of their existence) are actually of Costa-Rican origin. The only fact that supports my belief in their existence is the missionary's description of the unique amulet owned by the Jivaro chief.

This provokes another speculation. The tribe is known for its custom of keeping the mummified heads of their defeated enemies. It is a special art to crush the cranial bones of the severed head in such a way as to leave the skin unscathed, to extract the bone fragments and to fumigate the skull until it is reduced to the size of a fist—so that it can be then hung up as a trophy. This peculiar and savage custom suggests a certain connection between these trophies and the shape of that Jivaro amulet—provided that it was in fact produced locally. This, however, remains my personal theory, without concrete proofs. One can rely only on conjectures, and sum up the subject only by stating that the technique of jade carving in Central America must have borne great similarity to that of Stone Age China.

JADE CARVING IN NEW ZEALAND

The native population inhabiting the two South Pacific islands known as New Zealand are the Maoris, and there seems no doubt that their first habitations were on the North Island. They must have settled there around AD 1000, and created a characteristic civilisation of their own which is now being revealed by archaeological finds. It is, however, a complete mystery how they came to discover the rich alluvial deposits of nephritic jade, situated exclusively in the western region of the other, southern island. Jade is found there in the shape of fairly big pebbles, in two valleys protected by a towering mountain chain which could almost be called impassable. This region still is called 'the Green Country' or 'Jade Country'.

The trip of the Maori sailors in their fragile canoes across the stretch of stormy ocean to the South Island must have been long and perilous. It was made several centuries after their first landing on the North Island: in the more ancient layers of their excavations archaeologists have found only remnants of objects made of bone or ivory, but no jade whatsoever.

As a matter of fact, jade partly revolutionised the customs and habits of this race. While other civilisations used this stone to satisfy their urge for ornamental luxury, the Maoris turned it to more utilitarian purposes, making knives, hatchets and other tools, albeit primitive. These served their basic needs, enabling them to improve the quality of their woodwork as well as to build houses and canoes which they lovingly decorated with intricate carvings and totemistic ornaments.

Although New Zealand became an English colony in 1769, when Captain Cook took possession of the land on behalf of the British Crown, until about 150 years ago the Maoris led a Stone Age existence.

As they had no metals, the carving of jade (which in Maori language is known as 'pounamu') must have been a difficult task. It must be assumed that for this purpose they used sharp-edged pieces of jade itself, employing also in the process wetted quartz-containing sand which abounds on New Zealand beaches. At first the Maoris confined themselves to transporting the valuable stones to their home on the North Island, and working them there. To obtain them they would actually organise warlike expeditions to the South Island. Only later, it seems, did they occupy the other island too and arrange to work the jade where it was found. Still, the best of the ancient jade articles have been found on the North Island.

There is no indication that the belief in jade's

medicinal virtues so common in China ever took root among the Maoris. The almost reverential treatment of this mineral and the high value attached to it arose from the risks involved in obtaining it, as well as from its extreme hardness and the utility of the implements made with it.

Thus the very knives, hooks and other jade implements became the first adornments of the Maoris— worn on a string around the neck or attached to the bow of a canoe as talismans to ensure a good catch, since fish was the Maoris' staple food.

Among the ancient objects of the Maori civilisation there are two characteristic articles worthy of note. The 'mere' was a sort of mace or combat bludgeon which was at the same time the emblem of the chief and the symbol of authority. The 'hei-tiki' (cf. Plate 65), on the other hand, is a curious flat pendant whose shape was perhaps suggested by the hatchet. It is usually not longer than $2\frac{1}{2}$ to 3 inches and represents a strangely contorted human figure, apparently so shaped as to fit into a rectangle. The disproportionately large head is inclined to one side and rests directly on the shoulders without any neck, whilst the legs are contracted and connected to an arc which supports the body. There is also a coarsely engraved spiral-inspired decoration.

The symbolic significance of the hei-tiki is somewhat obscure. It is said to be a talisman and a representation of fecundity; on the other hand it also plays a part in certain funeral rites. In a certain sense it is an object of veneration similar to the ancestral tablets of the Chinese. At the death of a family head, his hei-tiki was buried with him. After the passing of a fixed period it was disinterred and then became an object of even more profound worship. Friends of the deceased gathered, formed a circle around the hei-tiki, and then intoned chants and funeral dirges.

The greatest technical problem for the ancient Maoris was always how to perforate a jade object so as to be able to append it. Some assert that they used for the purpose the same kind of primitive wooden drill as the ancient Chinese—that is, a wooden stick (instead of bamboo, which was not available) rotated with the help of a coiled cord drawn by a bow. It seems improbable, however, that they had such a contraption. A close scrutiny of the holes made in ancient Maori jade pieces clearly shows the obvious irregularities of their shape and leads to the conclusion that they were made by hand, very slowly, probably with the help of a pointed jade splinter and wet sand.

Today, in New Zealand as in China, jade is worked with carborundum drills and electrically propelled grindstones. Although the Chinese products are superior, the modern jade articles of New Zealand origin have their market and are very much in demand.

LIST OF ILLUSTRATIONS

1.   Pi disc with large central hole. Royal Shang tombs, Hsiao T'un (Anyang). Academy of Arts, Honolulu. Symbol of Heaven in ancient rituals which date back to China's Neolithic Age, i.e. to the period before the 2nd millennium BC. This specimen, devoid of any decorative element, is of earlier origin than the Anyang period and must have been several centuries old when it was buried (first half of the 2nd millennium BC).

2.   Dagger or sacrificial knife. Middle Shang period (16th-12th centuries BC). Academy of Arts, Honolulu. Short, thick blade made of clear nephritic jade, with bronze hilt richly decorated with the classical motifs typical of the bronze work of the period. The hole in the blade, designed for a cord on which to hang the object, is an indication that the function of the dagger was symbolic and ceremonial. Origin: Royal Shang Yin tombs in the region north-west of Anyang.

3.   Point of a ceremonial lance made of jade. Middle Shang period. Academy of Arts, Honolulu. Bronze handle inlaid with mosaic consisting of small slabs of turquoise. The staff, almost certainly made of a bamboo stick, has disappeared. Origin: excavations in the region of Anyang, the last capital of the Shang Dynasty. Typical of the artistic trend prevailing between the 14th and the 12th centuries BC.

4.   Ts'ung. Ritual symbol. Shang Yin period (12th to 11th centuries BC). Academy of Arts, Honolulu. Genuine nephritic jade with strong reddish specks. Symbolised the Earth-Goddess. This ritual object appears later in history than the Pi discs, which is understandable in view of the great difficulty of drilling a hole through the whole thickness of a boulder (to achieve the cylindrical shape) with the primitive tools of the time. Found at Hsiao T'un (Anyang), this Ts'ung is perhaps the oldest so far unearthed. All others of similar shape are made of softer materials.

138

5.   Pi disc in hatchet shape. Western Chou period (11th-8th centuries BC). British Museum, London. Ex Eumorfopoulos Collection. It symbolises perhaps the divine dualism Heaven-Earth, and is exceptional and unique. Dark-green nephritic jade with greyish and black veins.

6.   Strongly stylised human statuette. Late Chou or early Han period (4th-2nd centuries BC). British Museum, London. Ex Eumorfopoulos Collection. A priest or judge. Grey-green nephritic jade with brown and black spots.

7.   Hilt of a short ceremonial sword. Middle Chou period (9th-7th centuries BC). Museo Nazionale Orientale, Rome. Fiacchi-Gisondi Collection. Yellowish nephritic jade, strongly calcified. Even in archaic times jade was often used for handles or basket-hilts of short ceremonial swords which are typically Chinese.

8.   Ts'ung. Ritual symbol. Probably Warring States (481-221 BC). Victoria and Albert Museum, London. Nephritic jade. This remarkable precision in the carving of the very hard stone is undoubtedly indicative of considerable technical progress, and suggests a later date than the Chou period diagnosed by English experts.

9.　Ts'ung. Ritual symbol. Middle Chou period (9th-7th centuries BC). British Museum, London. Ex Eumorfopoulos Collection. Yellow nephritic jade with brown stripes. The flattened shape and certain irregularities in the central ribbing as well as in the incisions at the corners are fairly trustworthy clues to the object's date of origin.

10.　Basket-hilt of a short ceremonial sword. Warring States (481-221 BC). Museo Nazionale Orientale, Rome. Fiacchi-Gisondi Collection. Off-white nephritic jade. The symmetrical and semi-geometrical decoration is typical of the period. Origin: Honan.

11.　Chisels. Chou period (1122-256 BC). Museo Nazionale Orientale, Rome. Fiacchi-Gisondi Collection. Yellow nephritic jade. Complete absence of decoration makes the establishment of a more exact date impossible. Nevertheless, the shaped top of the smaller chisel (on the right in the reproduction) suggests that it is of a later date than the other, i.e. from the period between the 5th and the 3rd centuries BC. The other chisel could date back to the early Chou (11th-9th centuries BC).

12.　Ritual Pi disc. Warring States (481-221 BC). W. Rockhill Nelson Gallery of Art, Kansas City. Off-white nephritic jade with green veins. The exquisitely carved ornaments, consisting mainly of two mythical lions on the outside and one even more stylised on the inside, combine to create a work of singular beauty. There is some similarity to the specimen presented by the Chinese Government in 1935-1936 at the First Exhibition of Chinese Art in London.

13.   Pendant in dragon shape. Late Chou period. Museo Nazionale Orientale, Rome. Fiacchi-Gisondi Collection. White jade with brown speckles. The stylised serpentine shape of the object as well as the ornamental motif of spirals provides sufficient evidence for the date of origin: 5th-3rd centuries BC.

14.   Ritual Pi disc. Warring States (481-221 BC). W. Rockhill Nelson Gallery of Art, Kansas City. Green jade with brown spots (caused by iron impurities). The geometrical motif composed of exquisitely carved and highly stylised, intertwined dragons represents the culmination of jade-carving skill achieved by the ancient Chinese in this period. This masterpiece was certainly produced with the help of diamond drills.

15.   Pendant in stag shape. Late Chou period (4th-3rd centuries BC). Metropolitan Museum, New York. Rogers Fund. Off-white nephritic jade. The remarkable elegance with which the horns of the animal are shaped allows this object to be located to this period.

16.   Ancient safe-conducts. Middle Chou period (827-781 BC). Short cylinders made of brown jade, strongly calcified. From a drawing of the originals kept in a private collection in Peking.

17.   Sword-support for a belt. Warring States (481-221 BC).
Museo Nazionale Orientale, Rome. Fiacchi-Gisondi Collection.
White nephritic jade with brown specks. High-relief ornaments
represent stylised mythical animals.

18.   Hilt of a ceremonial sword. Warring States (481-221 BC).
Museo Nazionale Orientale, Rome. Fiacchi-Gisondi Collection.
White nephritic jade. The most outstanding feature of the
object is the neatly sculptured high-relief decoration in the
classical style of the 'intertwining motif' typical of the Warring
States period. Origin: Shensi.

19.   Ritual Pi disc. Warring States (481-221 BC). Museo
Nazionale Orientale, Rome. Fiacchi-Gisondi Collection. Off-
white nephritic jade. High-relief decoration with motifs of
stylised mythical animals.

20.   Ritual Pi disc. Warring States (481-221 BC). Museo
Nazionale Orientale, Rome. Fiacchi-Gisondi Collection. White
nephritic jade with green veins. Here too occurs the 'intertwining motif' mentioned previously as typical of the period.

21.   Stylised tiger, sculptured all round. Han period (206 BC-AD 220). Museo Poldi Pezzoli, Milan. Brown-speckled whitish jade. The Chinese artist responsible for this sculpture was certainly inspired by the uncommon colouring of the stone, the speckled surface seeming almost an imitation of a tiger's hide. (The spots are due to traces of ferric oxide or ferric silicate.)

22.   Horse head. Han period (206 BC - AD 220). Victoria and Albert Museum, London. Plain light-green jade. Although this sculpture incontestably bears the stylistic mark of the Han period, the exaggerated bend of the neck and the lack of dynamic expressiveness (a characteristic of the period's climax) suggests a date of origin not earlier than 2nd century AD.

23.   Disc in greenish-white jade, with black dots. Han period (206 BC-AD 220). Museo Nazionale Orientale, Rome. Fiacchi-Gisondi Collection. The circular incision in the centre is due to an attempt (obviously interrupted) aimed at turning the object into a Pi disc. The other side (not visible in the reproduction) is completely covered with ornaments consisting of little spirals. Although the circular cut has not been completed, it is interesting in so far as it is clearly vertical and not slanted, which indicates the use of a tool different from the habitual bone or bamboo drill.

24.   Pendant in hatchet shape. Han period (206 BC-AD 220). Museo Nazionale Orientale, Rome. Fiacchi-Gisondi Collection. Greyish nephritic jade with black veins. In its upper part the specimen has lightly carved decorations consisting of parallel stripes and a central semi-geometrical motif with little spirals. Origin: Honan.

25. Double belt-buckle. Han period (206 BC-AD 220). Private Collection, Milan. Ex Fiacchi-Gisondi Collection. Jade with black veins. Although the rudimentary carving on the clasp is the object's only decoration, the buckle is impressive in the elegance of its finish and the perfect fit of its two curved halves.

26. Ritual Pi disc. Han period (206 BC-AD 220). Museo Nazionale Orientale, Rome. Fiacchi-Gisondi Collection. White, slightly translucent jade. The relief ornaments carved on the disc's circumference consist of eight classical 'trigrammes' (series of three lines—either intact or broken—in all possible combinations) which in their totality (Pa-Kua) represent the integrity of the Cosmic Universe.

27. Pendant: serpent-like dragon. British Museum, London. Off-white nephritic jade. Although this specimen has been classified as dating back to the Six Dynasties period (AD 265-589), it is more likely to originate from the Sung period (AD 960-1279).

28. Mythological monster. T'ang period (AD 618-906). Museo Nazionale Orientale, Rome. Fiacchi-Gisondi Collection. Greenish nephritic jade with brown speckles. This kind of animal statuette, carved out of alluvial pebbles, had no utilitarian purpose but was obviously used as a trinket in accordance with the prevailing fashion of the T'ang period.

29. Duck or other bird. T'ang period (AD 618-906). British Museum, London. Ex Eumorfopoulos Collection. Dark-brown nephritic jade with traces of varnish baked on natural red pigments.

30. Duck, carved in the round. T'ang period (AD 618-906). Museo Poldi Pezzoli, Milan. Yellowish jade. Roundish shapes of this kind are typical of the small-size T'ang figures. It is worth noting that animals were as a rule represented in a crouching position.

31. Goat-like animal. T'ang period (AD 618-906). Museo Nazionale Orientale, Rome. Fiacchi-Gisondi Collection. Nephritic jade. The rotundity and diminutive size of such objects (which easily fitted the palm of the hand) suggests that their purpose was not only decorative: they were believed to cure or prevent certain ailments merely by contact with the skin.

32. Crouching animal. T'ang period (AD 618-906). Museo Poldi Pezzoli, Milan. Sculptured all round out of a yellow nephrite pebble with reddish specks. The caparison, sketchily incised on the animal's back, and the trunk-like snout (folded up against the body) suggest that the unknown Chinese artist might have intended to portray a resting elephant.

33. Goblet for festive occasions. Sung period (AD 960-1279). Victoria and Albert Museum, London. White jade with greenish-brown specks. The body,of the vessel is decorated with mythological animals in high-relief and in bas-relief. The handle is in the shape of a stylised dragon. Perhaps made in the first half of the 12th century.

34. Pendant in small hatchet shape. Sung period (AD 960-1279). Museo Nazionale Orientale, Rome. Fiacchi-Gisondi Collection. Yellowish jade. The top is sculptured in dragon shape, while the upper part is decorated with a strip of lightly carved archaic motifs.

35. Cylindrical bracelet. Sung period (AD 960-1279). Museo Nazionale Orientale, Rome. Fiacchi-Gisondi Collection. White-brown jade. On its outer side this bracelet shows ornaments carved in high-relief.

36. Pendant with mythological animals. Sung period (AD 960-1279). Museo Nazionale Orientale, Rome. Fiacchi-Gisondi Collection. Nephritic white jade with dark-brown veins. The stylised mythological animals appear at the top and on one of the side edges of this specimen.

37. Cylindrical receptacle for washing paint-brushes. Sung period (AD 960-1279). Museo Poldi Pezzoli, Milan. Grey jade with strong brownish specks. Noteworthy is the archaic style decoration carved in two parallel strips. It consists of highly stylised animal figures, distinguished by neat and precise outlines.

38. Bowl. Sung period (AD 960-1279). Museo Poldi Pezzoli, Milan. Greyish nephrite. The neatly carved ornaments on the outside of the bowl consist of a 'Greek frieze' (Lei Wen) around the rim, while the rest of the body is covered with a regular geometrical pattern of spirals which follow each other vertically.

39. Crescent-shaped plaque. Sung period (AD 960-1279). Musée Guimet, Paris. Green jade. The two ends of the crescent have the shape of dragon heads which face each other. Also noteworthy is the meticulously carved pattern of fish scales, certainly achieved only through infinite patience. A typical piece of the Sung period.

40. Mythical monster, sculptured all round. Probably late Sung. Museo Poldi Pezzoli, Milan. White jade with brown veins. The somewhat rudimentary workmanship of this piece has little in common with the refinement of the 12th century. Hence the strong suspicion that it was made at the end of the Sung period (13th century).

41. Receptacle in shape of ritual archaic bronze (Kuei). Yüan or early Ming period. Academy of Arts, Honolulu. The decoration faithfully follows the pattern of bronze-work in the Middle Chou period (9th to 7th centuries BC), but the origin of this jade object is much later: either the beginning of the Ming period (AD 1368-1644) or the Yüan period (AD 1280-1368).

42. Bowl. Ming period (AD 1368-1644). British Museum, London. Ex Eumorfopoulos Collection. The 'swinging handle' is carved from the same piece of jade as the bowl. Carved in pale grey-green jade, the vessel delights the eye by its perfect form, despite the comparatively thick walls. Classified as belonging to the Ming period, the bowl could possibly have been made somewhat earlier, in the Yüan period (AD 1280-1368).

43. Big tortoise. Ming period (AD 1368-1644). British Museum, London. Grey-green nephrite (the 'cabbage jade' of the Chinese). This specimen's exceptional dimensions (52 centimetres) lead to the conclusion that during the Ming period the import of nephritic jade from Khotan into China was no longer confined to alluvial pebbles but included also huge blocks obtained from quarries. Certainly the beginnings of jade extraction from rocks date back to the 11th or 12th century.

44. Cicada-shaped pendant. Ming period (AD 1368-1644). Museo Nazionale Orientale, Rome. Fiacchi-Gisondi Collection. White jade with brownish-black specks. Thanks to the anatomical accuracy of this creation and its superb workmanship (of unusual precision), this small object can be considered a veritable gem among jades.

45. Big fish, possibly a carp. Ming period (AD 1368-1644). Museo Poldi Pezzoli, Milan. White jade. This is one of many examples of various animals accurately portrayed in jade (sometimes of considerable dimensions), a fashion in the Ming period.

46. An Immortal meditating in a grotto. Ming period (AD 1368-1644). Metropolitan Museum, New York. Sculptured in nephritic jade, this specimen is clearly inspired by the Tao cult. It was probably produced during the reign of Emperor Chia Ching (AD 1521-1567) who, in contrast to all his predecessors, was a fervent Taoist.

47. Pendant in sounding-stone shape. Ch'ing period. Museo Nazionale Orientale, Rome. Fiacchi-Gisondi Collection. White jade with brown specks. This is a remarkable example of decorative refinement. Reign of Ch'ien Lung (AD 1736-1795).

48. Bowl. Ch'ing period (AD 1644-1911). Victoria and Albert Museum, London. The two 'swinging handles' were carved from the same piece of jade as the vessel, in nephritic jade. A good example of carved and sculptured ornaments inspired by archaic style. The finesse of the 'Greek Motif' (Lei Wen) suggests that the work was executed with tools with diamond or corundum tips.

49.   Belt buckle. Ch'ing period. Museo Nazionale Orientale, Rome. Fiacchi-Gisondi Collection. Brown jade. The relief sculpture executed with high precision is a typical example of the advanced technique of Chinese jade craftsmen in the 18th century. Reign of Ch'ien Lung (AD 1736-1795).

50.   Bowl with lid. Ch'ing period. Victoria and Albert Museum, London. Made of remarkably translucent greenish-white nephritic jade. Here the ornaments are partly sculptured and partly carved in filigree, thus achieving an exquisite effect on the vessel's lid. Reign of Ch'ien Lung (AD 1736-1795).

51.   Hsi Wang Mu accompanied by a phoenix. Ch'ing period. Victoria and Albert Museum, London. White jade. The translucent quality of the material endows the delicate female figure (the mythical Queen of the West) with suggestive beauty. End of 18th century AD.

52.   Small group of personages. Ch'ing period. Victoria and Albert Museum, London. W. H. Cape legacy. White nephritic jade. Minute little figures, sculptured all round, crowd round a bigger central figure, thus suggesting a movement towards the centre. 18th century.

53. Sculptured panel: the Immortals in a retreat. Ch'ing period. Victoria and Albert Museum, London. Wells legacy. White jade. This panel was probably part of a piece of furniture or a small table screen. Attributed to the 18th century.

54. Medallion or garment button. Ch'ing period (AD 1644-1911). Victoria and Albert Museum, London. Wells legacy. The relief sculpture represents a dragon among clouds. It probably belongs to the end of the 18th century, i.e. late Ch'ien Lung.

55. Round jade medallion. Ch'ing period. Victoria and Albert Museum, London. The finely sculptured decoration covers the whole surface of the medallion and represents the Eight Immortals in the Taoist Empyrean, probably the Island of Happiness. On the reverse of the medallion there is a representation of Lao Tse (the Old Child). Reign of Ch'ien Lung (AD 1736-1795).

56. Sauce-boat in shape of archaic ritual bronze. Ch'ing period. Museo Poldi Pezzoli, Milan. Greyish jade. This specimen is one of the many and various objects of the period which re-create the shapes and decorative motifs of classical bronzes. Reign of Ch'ien Lung (AD 1736-1795).

57. Two ceremonial sceptres (Ju I). Ch'ing period. Museo Nazionale Orientale, Rome. Fiacchi-Gisondi Collection. The sceptre reproduced on the right is made of greenish nephritic jade, the other of lively green Burma jadeite. They both date back to the Ch'ien Lung period (AD 1736-1795), but the sceptre first mentioned is almost certainly a few decades older than the other.

58. Jar with lid marked Ch'ien Lung. Ch'ing period. Museo Poldi Pezzoli, Milan. Intense-green jadeite. Exquisite ornaments superbly executed. An important object, marked Ch'ien Lung (AD 1736-1795) and in fact belonging to this period. Originally it was used in an Imperial palace.

59. Sculptured plaque representing a deity. Maya art. American Museum of Natural History, New York. Probably from a region of Mexico, and not from Yucatan, the cradle of the Maya civilisation (4th-6th centuries AD).

60. Statuette of a seated man. Maya art. Museo Nacional de Antropología, Mexico City. Nephritic jade. This figure, probably representing a wise man (or at any rate an important personage), possesses all the characteristics of the best Maya sculptures. 14th-15th century AD.

61. Human mask in mosaic made of jade fragments. Maya art. Museo Nacional de Antropología, Mexico City. Because of its remarkable expressive power and the originality of its overall conception this mask is a classical sample of the Maya art of the 14th and 15th centuries AD.

62. Breast-plate worn at ritual ceremonies. Zapotec civilisation (3rd-2nd century BC). Museo Nacional de Antropología, Mexico City. This represents the mask of a God, and was used by Shaman priests of a particular type. The two holes at the sides are meant for a cord with which to hang the breast-plate round the neck.

63. Statuette of 'dragon', sculptured all round. Ancient Olmec art (8th-5th centuries BC). American Museum of Natural History, New York. Green jadeite with yellow specks. Dragon or another mythological animal sculptured out of a single jadeite block.

64. Statuette of weeping child, sculptured all round. Olmeca art. Museo Nacional de Antropología, Mexico City. Green jadeite pebble. Despite its intentional classical simplicity it provides an excellent example of the expressive power so typical of Olmec art (3rd-1st century BC).

65. Hei-tiki amulet. Maori art. Museo Pigorini, Rome. Coarsely carved out of a nephritic jade pebble. A strange pendant-amulet. The eyes have been made more prominent by circles of red lacquer. Belongs probably to the period between the 16th and 17th centuries AD.